Roots above and
Warm quiet earth at my side,
Wildflowers spread the word:
Sun's mission is succeeding.

— Wyaye Wenundar

MALCOLM WELLS
Underground Designs

Distributed by Brick House Publishing Co.
Andover, Mass.

Malcolm Wells, architect and author, has worked for four years now in his own sunny, underground office. He is author of Energy Essays and co-author of Your Home's Solar Potential and Solaria.

Editing and Book Design by David Deppen
Compilation of Technical Sections by David Deppen

Library of Congress Cataloging in Publication Data

Wells, Malcolm.
    Underground designs.

    Reprint of the ed. published by the author, Brewster, MA.
    Includes index.
    1. Underground architecture—United States.   I. Title
NA2542.7.W44   1981   720   81-184
ISBN 0-931790-20-4   AACR1

This book was written and published underground.

Our climate is of the four-seasons, hot-summer, cold-winter, 40-inch-per-year-rainfall variety. Most of the designs in this book are based on those conditions, so be sure to get good local advice if you plan to build in an area where the conditions are different.

I hope the designs that follow encourage you in the direction of earth-covered construction. Feel free to develop schemes in the spirit of the designs shown here. If you are interested in building a specific project or part of a project as shown here, please write to me for permission.

— Malcolm Wells

Harriet's Lesson

More than 5000 people have written to us requesting information on underground buildings. Back in the mid-Sixties, when such letters arrived at the rate of only one or two a month (we were lucky to get that many!) we answered them individually, but as the numbers grew we had to resort to using form letters, which seemed to satisfy some of our correspondents, but most people wanted more variety, more detail, more answers than a stock response could offer.

That's why we prepared this book. It's still a stock response, of course, but it seems fairer to both buyer and seller. You get more information, and we get money for preparing it.

This is mainly a collection of drawings — underground designs — for buildings still mostly unbuilt, drawn during the past thirteen years. If some of these early designs had been built, the results could have been a real problem, but now, thanks largely to our experiences in this experimental office, we've begun to understand some of the natural phenomena involved in this new/old way of building. We've marked many of the drawings with comments on this new understanding.

My first decision, back in 1964, was to admit sunlight to all inhabitable underground spaces. That was the best idea of all, deciding to avoid the dungeon approach to subterranean architecture. If I was going underground to make more living space for the creatures of the natural world, I was at least going to take a lot of sunlight with me. I wanted real windows and real views, real fresh air and real breezes; none of that electronic stuff.

The easiest way to get the real thing is to build into a hillside, and many of my designs use that idea. Another way is to have rooms overlooking a sunken garden or courtyard, and many of my designs use that idea, too. Then, once real sunlight and fresh air were assured, I got more deeply into my designs by building my underground office, hoping to avoid any unpleasant surprises nature might have had in store for me down here.

In a very basic sense there were no surprises at all. The natural laws that govern all things above ground govern all things below. Falling objects fall just the same, water still runs downhill, and heated air continues to rise. Nevertheless, it took some embarrassing little disasters to teach me the ground rules. The underground rules.

I hadn't used my head. I hadn't even used my rear end. Decades of spring days spent chilling it sitting too long on cool, damp soil hadn't prepared me for the endless heat-loss I'd have through these uninsulated walls. I thought earth was all the insulation I needed. I thought earth temperatures everywhere were exactly the same. Well, even my Aunt Harriet could have told me differently.

A few feet from where I sit, hundreds of tons of wet New Jersey soil are quietly draining the warmth from this room. They're doing it very slowly, I'll admit, but it seems now as if they'll go on doing it forever. I get up and put another small log on the slow-buring woodstove, and the chill goes away. Six or eight hours will have to pass, now, before the earth catches up again. Outside, in the sunlit courtyard, a starling is arguing with a cardinal.

This building uses far less fuel, even without insulation, than does a comparable above-ground building — less, even, than a well-insulated above-ground building. But oh, how I wish I'd used some insulation! Nowadays, we use it all the time. With insulation to stop most of a room's heat-loss, and a huge earth mass all around to resist the icy gales outside, the spaces in our newer buildings need very little fuel — sometimes none at all, when solar heat is used. But, we'll get into all that later on. What I want to say here is that I really think we're onto something.

When Popular Mechanics published a feature on underground architecture, in March 1977, the mail response was the largest in the company's history. When we publicized Underground America Day (May 14) our incoming mail looked as heavy as Popular Mechanics' for a while. We were swamped! We couldn't understand it. Was it because of the Great Winter of '77? Was it the appealing design of some of the underground buildings people had seen? Was it a longing for the warmth and security of the womb? Was it the growing disgust with the asphalting of America? Or was it some lingering primal force in us? After all, man lived in caves for a long time.

Is there still some undetected human impulse that tells us this way is right? — that tells us, in spite of all our acquired phobias, that this is the place to build? I'll gladly leave that question to the psychologists, but I think this really is the place. We can have fragrant, silent cities and towns under miles of trees and wildflowers instead of endless asphalt and concrete — cities and towns that benefit from, rather than disintegrate under, the forces of nature. This will happen not just by going underground, of course, but by our seeing what's really happening around us, and trying to respond to it more appropriately.

SUNNY HOMES

"It's early Saturday morning, before the crowds arrive. These earth-covered model homes express two versions of the <u>sun/earth theme</u>." — that's how I introduced this <u>sketch</u> to the builder who wants <u>clusters</u> of them....

.... all situated on a gently-sloping south-facing hillside in New Jersey. Both houses are designed for <u>multiple construction</u>.

NORTH

6

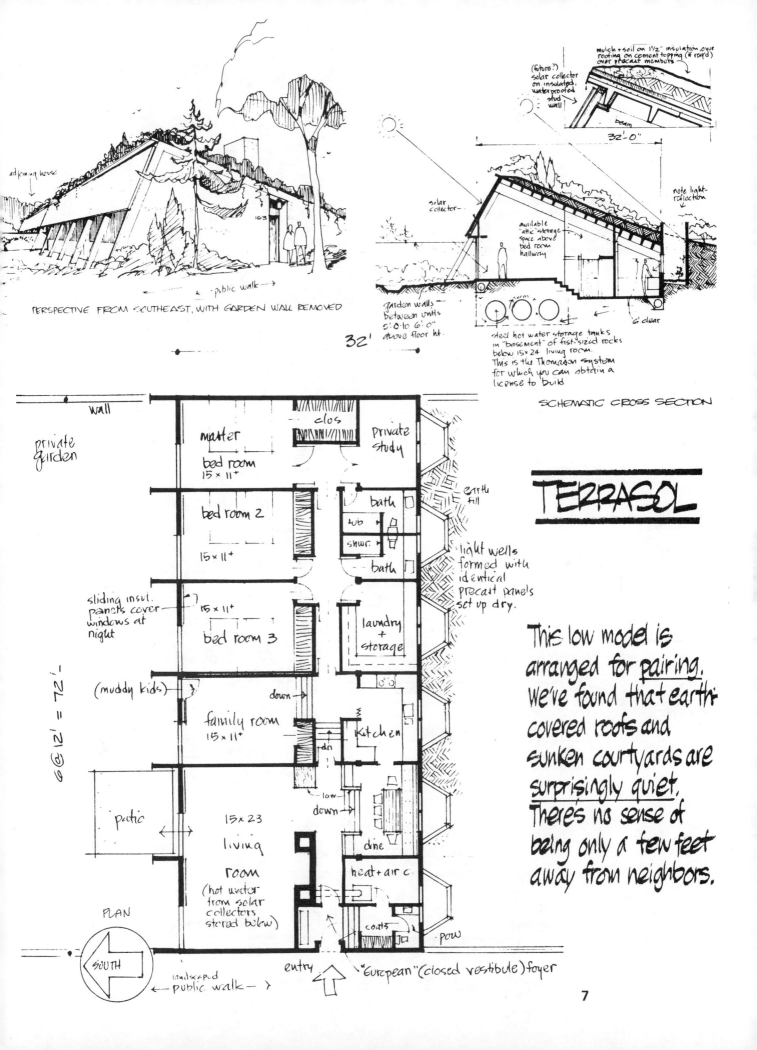

PERSPECTIVE FROM SOUTHEAST, WITH GARDEN WALL REMOVED

adjoining house

← public walk →

163

32'

mulch + soil on 1½" insulation over roofing on cement topping (if req'd) over precast members

(future?) solar collector on insulated, waterproofed stud wall

beam

32'-0"

note light reflection

solar collector

available "attic" storage space above bed room hallway

garden walls between units 5'-0" to 6'-0" above floor ht.

warm

6' clear

steel hot water storage tanks in "basement" of fist-sized rocks below 15 x 24 living room. This is the Thomason system for which you can obtain a license to build

SCHEMATIC CROSS SECTION

PLAN

wall

private garden

master bed room 15 × 11+

clos

Private study

bed room 2

15 × 11+

bath

tub

shwr.

bath

sliding insul. panels cover windows at night

15 × 11+

bed room 3

laundry + storage

earth fill

light wells formed with identical precast panels set up dry.

(muddy kids)

down →

family room 15 × 11+

dn

Kitchen

6 @ 12' = 72'

low →

patio

down →

15 × 23 living room (hot water from solar collectors stored below)

dine

heat + air c

coats

pow

SOUTH

entry

"European" (closed vestibule) foyer

landscaped ← public walk →

TERRASOL

This low model is arranged for pairing. We've found that earth covered roofs and sunken courtyards are surprisingly quiet. There's no sense of being only a few feet away from neighbors.

FRONT STREET

12" of mulch { leaves, pine needles, grass cuttings, pulled weeds, etc

6" topsoil

12" subsoil

6" layer of pebbles { waterproofing and insulation

8" flat slab

continuous drip-edge

8" block masonry

-24" columns @ 12'-0" oc made of 8" block

tough cement plaster on insulation

carpet on 4" reinf. slab over plastic sheet + 4" pebbles

7'-4"

2'-0"

WALL SECTION

Because of the owner's insistence upon having <u>garage doors</u> on what he considered to be the front of this house, we had to shoehorn it onto the lot. In open sunlight this might have been a more serious problem. Here the <u>tree-shaded lot</u> made solar orientation less important.

notice exterior insulation wraps roof, overhangs, and walls

existing grade

door to bed rooms

<u>CROSS SECTION THROUGH LIVING-PIT-KITCHEN</u>

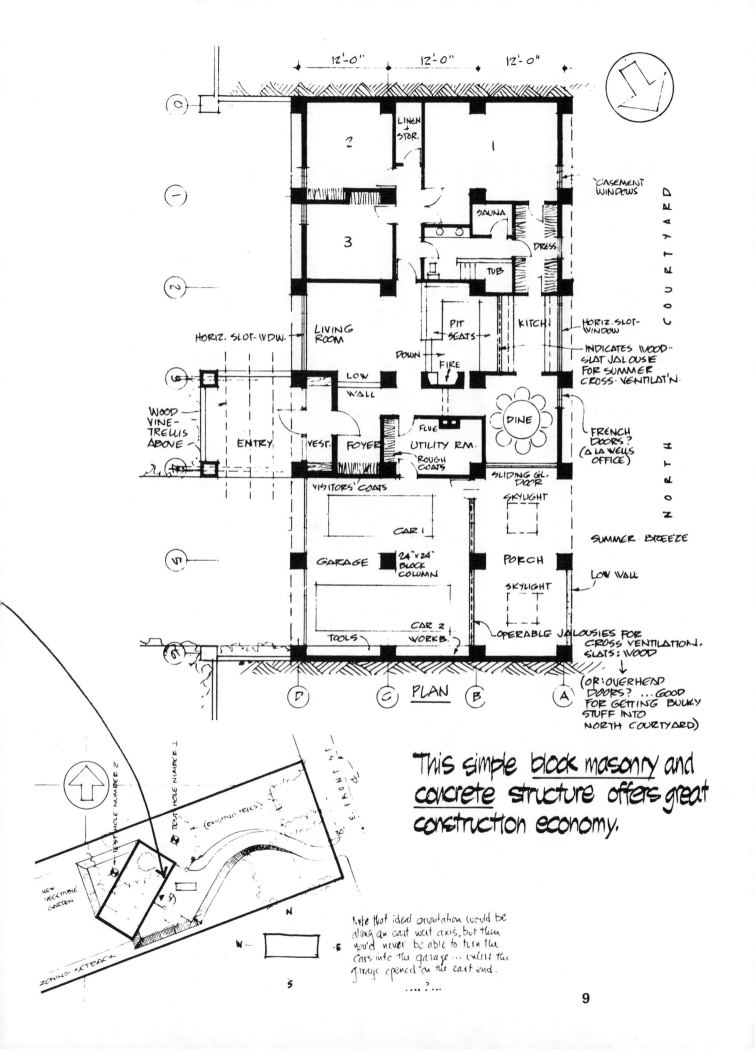

All through the <u>winter of '77</u> we waited for word from the Homans. January. February. March... Finally Bob visited us and we all said, "Well?"

"We <u>didn't</u> use the auxiliary heat at all."

So we had our first real proof, that under record conditions, <u>solar heat and earth cover</u> is a powerful combination, even in the Northeastern part of the United States.

10

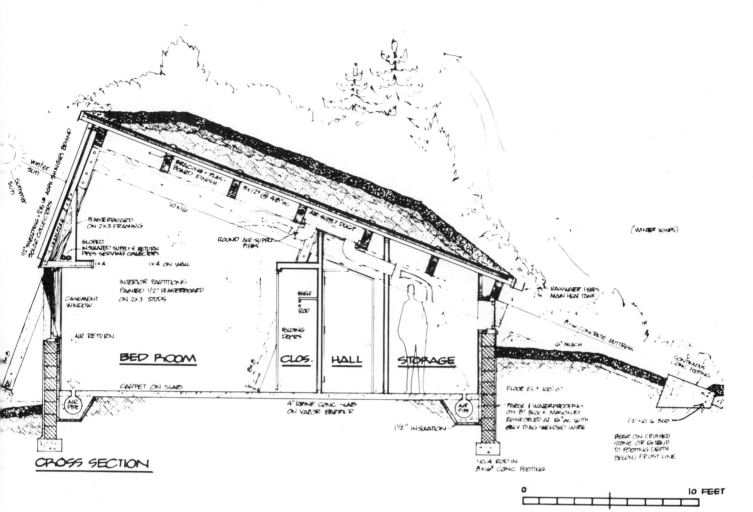

CROSS SECTION

Labels in the cross section diagram:
- winter sun
- summer sun
- 1/2" SHEATHING, .06# ASPH SHINGLES BEHIND
- SOLAR COLLECTORS
- BRACING + PLAS-BOARD FINISH
- 5x12 @ 48"oc
- 10x16
- AIR SUPPLY DUCT
- PLASTERBOARD ON 2x3 FRAMING
- ROUND AIR SUPPLY PIPES
- SLOPED, INSULATED SUPPLY & RETURN PIPES SERVING COLLECTORS
- 1x4
- 1x4 ON WALL
- (WINTER WINDS)
- INTERIOR PARTITIONS PAINTED 1/2" PLASTERBOARD ON 2x3 STUDS
- SHELF + ROD
- RAINWATER FEEDS MAIN HEAT TANK
- CASEMENT WINDOW
- AIR RETURN
- FOLDING DOORS
- 6" CONCRETE BUTTRESS
- 6" MULCH
- CONTINUOUS CONC FOOTING
- **BED ROOM**
- **CLOS.**
- **HALL**
- **STORAGE**
- CARPET ON SLAB
- FLOOR EL + 100'-0"
- 4" REINF CONC SLAB ON VAPOR BARRIER
- AIR PIPE
- AIR PIPE
- 1 1/2" INSULATION
- PARGE & WATERPROOFING ON 8" BLOCK MASONRY REINFORCED AT 16"oc WITH GALV DIAG-WELDED WIRE
- (2) NO 6 BED
- BEAR ON CRUSHED STONE, OR EXTEND TO FOOTING DEPTH BELOW FROST LINE
- NO. 4 ROD IN 8x16" CONC FOOTING

0 ————— 10 FEET

Until they're reminded of the way the ceilings of mines are supported, people are skeptical about supporting earth with <u>wood.</u> In a properly designed structure the two are an ideal combination.

This house is based on a design theme so simple, we've done <u>dozens of variations</u> on it and dozens more are possible.

Location: Suburban Philadelphia

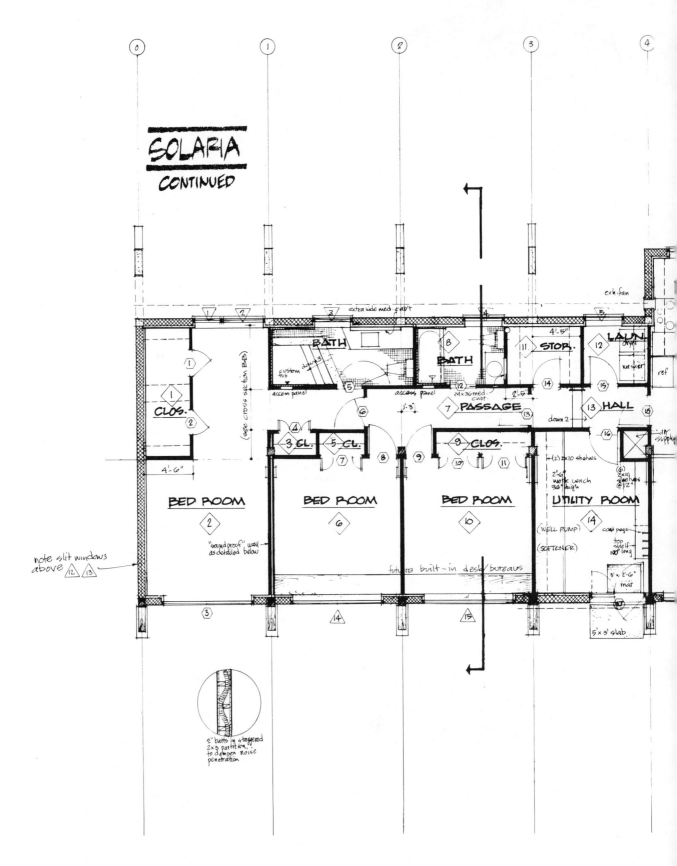

SOLARIA
CONTINUED

note slit windows above 12 13

BED ROOM 2
"sound proof" wall as detailed below

CLOS.

BED ROOM 6

BED ROOM 10

UTILITY ROOM 14
(WELL PUMP)
(SOFTENER)

BATH

BATH

PASSAGE

STOR.

LAUN dryer

HALL

washer

ref

2" batts in staggered 2x3 partition to dampen noise penetration

future built-in desk/bureaus

We saved the owners space and money by using trapdoors to the utility space below, but a stairway down to a bonafide basement would have been an improvement on this plan.

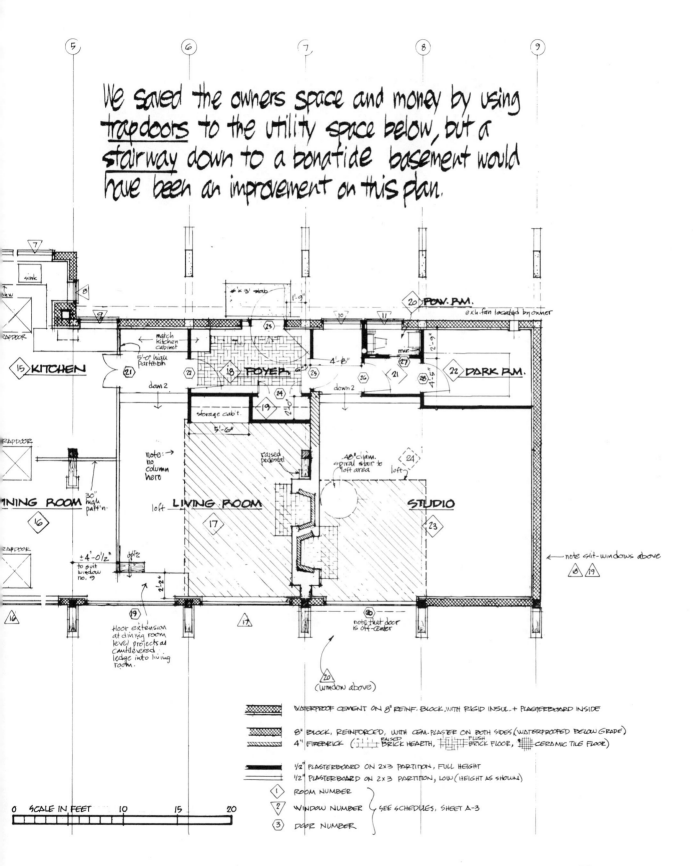

WATERPROOF CEMENT ON 8" REINF. BLOCK. WITH RIGID INSUL.+ PLASTERBOARD INSIDE

8" BLOCK, REINFORCED, WITH CEM. PLASTER ON BOTH SIDES (WATERPROOFED BELOW GRADE)

4" FIREBRICK (⊞⊞ RAISED BRICK HEARTH, ⊞⊞ FLUSH BRICK FLOOR, ⊞⊞ CERAMIC TILE FLOOR)

½" PLASTERBOARD ON 2x3 PARTITION, FULL HEIGHT

½" PLASTERBOARD ON 2x3 PARTITION, LOW (HEIGHT AS SHOWN)

① ROOM NUMBER
▽ WINDOW NUMBER — SEE SCHEDULES, SHEET A-3
◇ DOOR NUMBER

0 SCALE IN FEET   10   15   20

13

PROPERTY LINES

PRIVACY SCREEN

VICTORIA AVENUE

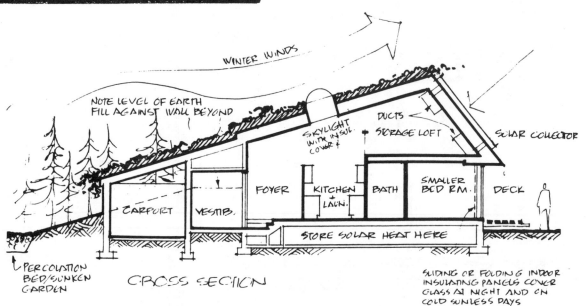

WINTER WINDS

NOTE LEVEL OF EARTH FILL AGAINST WALL BEYOND

SKYLIGHT WITH INSUL COVER

DUCTS

STORAGE LOFT

SOLAR COLLECTOR

CARPORT   VESTIB.   FOYER   KITCHEN + LAUN.   BATH   SMALLER BED RM.   DECK

STORE SOLAR HEAT HERE

PERCOLATION BED/SUNKEN GARDEN

CROSS SECTION

SLIDING OR FOLDING INDOOR INSULATING PANELS COVER GLASS AT NIGHT AND ON COLD SUNLESS DAYS

These houses carry the sun/earth theme a step further: sun/earth/rain. Each roof slopes down into a percolation bed—a sunken garden that becomes part of the endless landscape. Also—the porous paver blocks of the driveway further reduce wasteful runoff.

14

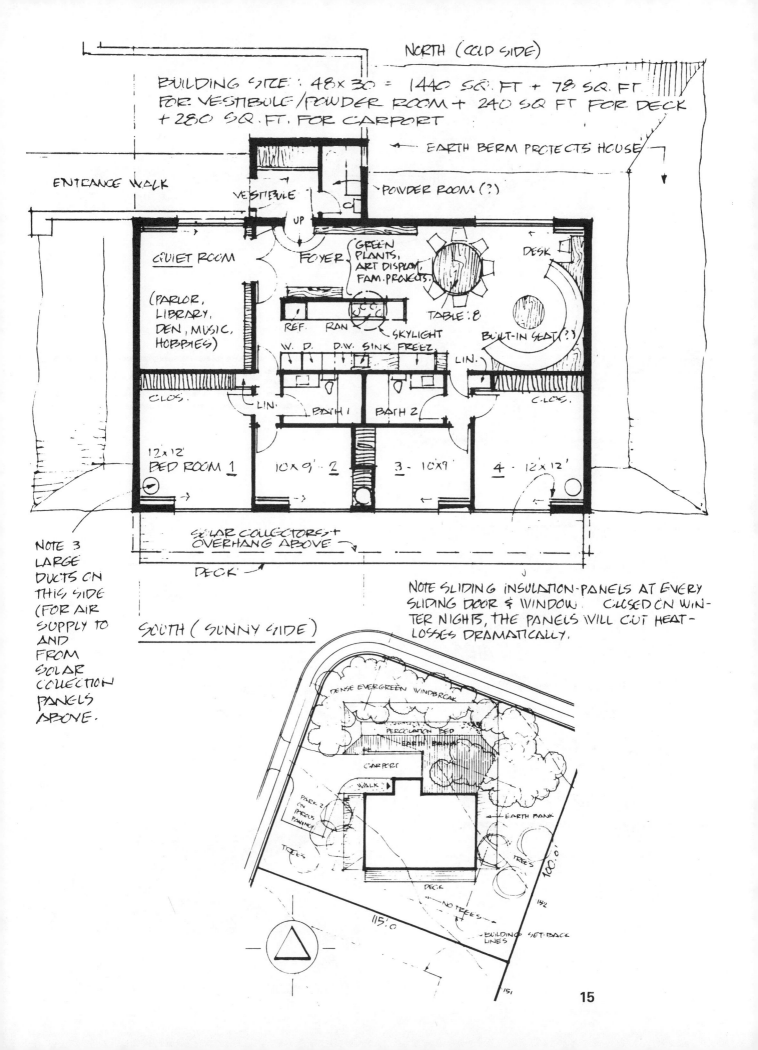

BUILDING SIZE: 48x30 = 1440 SQ. FT + 78 SQ. FT
FOR VESTIBULE/POWDER ROOM + 240 SQ FT FOR DECK
+ 280 SQ. FT. FOR CARPORT

← EARTH BERM PROTECTS HOUSE

ENTRANCE WALK

VESTIBULE

→ POWDER ROOM (?)

UP

QUIET ROOM

FOYER

GREEN PLANTS, ART DISPLAY, FAM. PROJECTS.

DESK

(PARLOR, LIBRARY, DEN, MUSIC, HOBBIES)

REF. RAN

SKYLIGHT

TABLE: 8

BUILT-IN SEAT (?)

W. D. D.W. SINK FREEZ.

LIN.

CLOS.

LIN.

BATH 1

BATH 2

CLOS.

12x12'
BED ROOM 1

10x9' 2

3 · 10'x9'

4 · 12x12'

NOTE 3 LARGE DUCTS ON THIS SIDE (FOR AIR SUPPLY TO AND FROM SOLAR COLLECTION PANELS ABOVE.

SOLAR COLLECTORS + OVERHANG ABOVE →

DECK

SOUTH (SUNNY SIDE)

NOTE SLIDING INSULATION-PANELS AT EVERY SLIDING DOOR & WINDOW. CLOSED ON WINTER NIGHTS, THE PANELS WILL CUT HEAT-LOSSES DRAMATICALLY.

DENSE EVERGREEN WINDBREAK

PERCOLATION BED

EARTH BANK

CARPORT

WALK

PARK 2 ON POROUS PAVING

EARTH BANK

TREES

TREES

DECK

NO TREES

100.0'

152

BUILDING SET-BACK LINES

115.0'

151

15

house, as seen
from the cul-de-sac

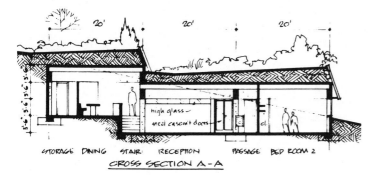

STORAGE DINING STAIR RECEPTION   PASSAGE BED ROOM 2

CROSS SECTION A-A

high glass
steel casem't doors
cl

THE MINOT HOUSE

The water-trapping profile of the lower roof shown above is misleading. Actually the water drains easily from the low area into the courtyards. The parapet walls shown to hold back the earth are a part of this design I'd now recommend be avoided. The pressures on them from freezing causes problems.

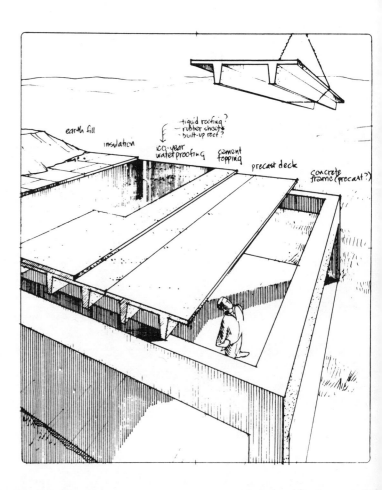

earth fill

insulation

liquid roofing?
rubber sheet?
built-up roof?

100-year
water proofing

cement
topping

precast deck

concrete
frame (precast?)

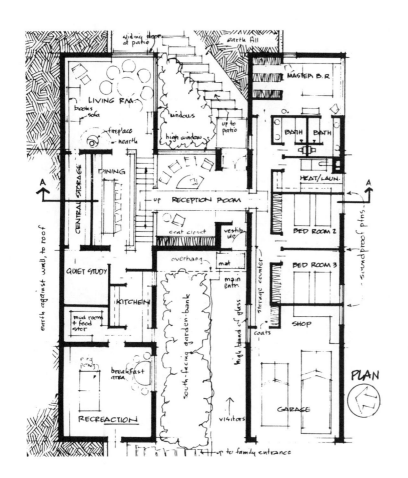

PLAN

You can imagine what the winters are like in <u>Northern North Dakota</u>. They gave us further reason to burrow into the sheltering earth. That led us to this <u>two level</u> design. Solar heat storage: below the floor.

Living room area labels: sliding door at patio, earth fill, LIVING RM., books, sofa, fireplace, hearth, windows, high window, up to patio, MASTER B.R., BATH, BATH, CENTRAL STORAGE, DINING, up, RECEPTION ROOM, HEAT/LAUN., earth against wall, to roof, coat closet, vestibule, BED ROOM 2, soundproof ptns., overhang, mat, main entr., QUIET STUDY, KITCHEN, storage counter, BED ROOM 3, mud room + feed stor, coats, SHOP, dog pens, breakfast area, south-facing garden-bank, high band of glass, RECREACTION, visitors, GARAGE, up to family entrance

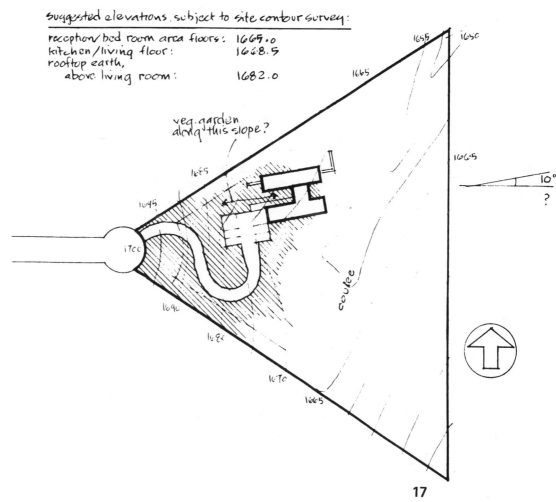

suggested elevations, subject to site contour survey:

reception/bed room area floors:	1665.0
kitchen/living floor:	1668.5
rooftop earth, above living room:	1682.0

veg. garden along this slope?

coulee

10° ?

1700

1655 1650 1665 1666.5 1665 1645 1690 1685 1670 1665

ENTRANCE

Designed in 1964, this first underground design of mine was never built, and yet it has been by far the most popular and widely published house I've ever designed.
I'd do it differently today, of course. There would be larger windows facing south and the insulation would be on the outside for greater thermal efficiency but I'd certainly try to keep the inviting, earthy freedom I stumbled upon here.

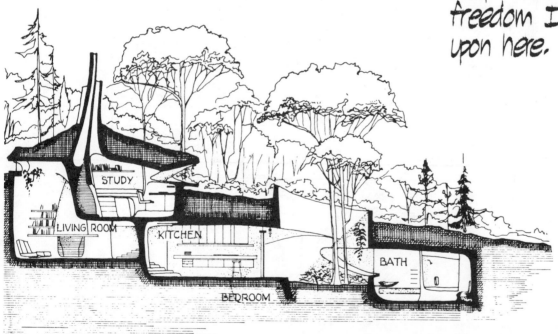

STUDY

LIVING ROOM

KITCHEN

BATH

BEDROOM

A RANDOM HOUSE

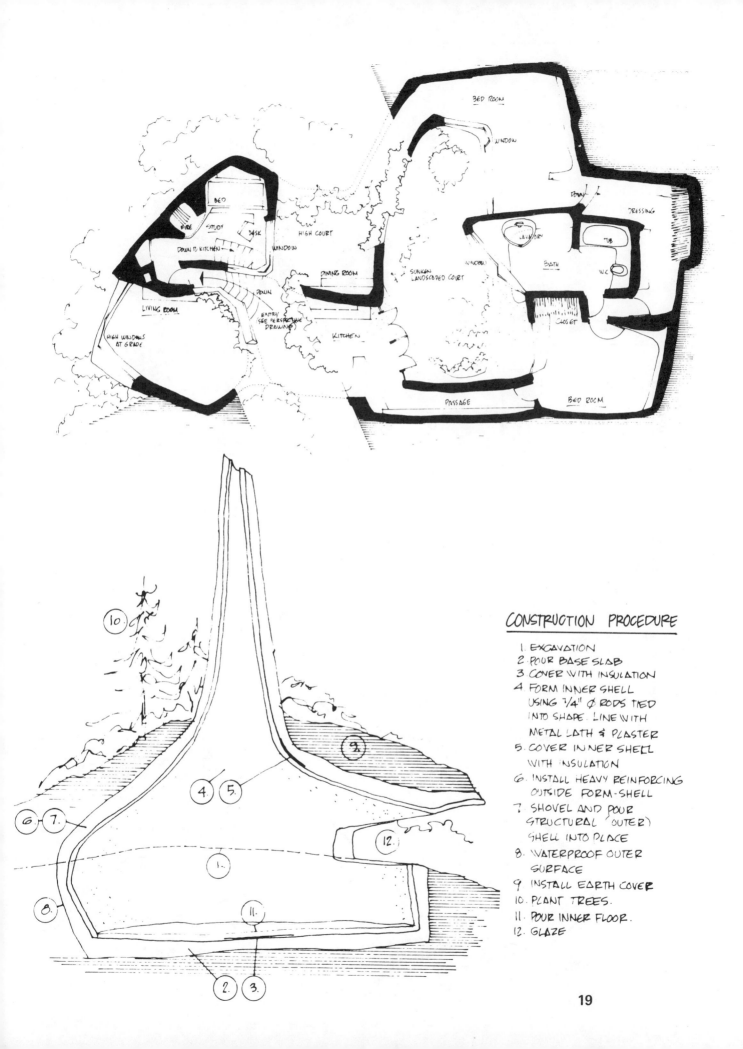

BED ROOM

WINDOW

DOWN

DRESSING

BED

FIRE

STUDY

DESK

HIGH COURT

DOWN TO KITCHEN

WINDOW

LAVATORY

TUB

BATH

WC

DINING ROOM

SUNKEN LANDSCAPED COURT

WINDOW

DOWN

LIVING ROOM

ENTRY SEE PERSPECTIVE DRAWING

CLOSET

HIGH WINDOWS AT GRADE

KITCHEN

PASSAGE

BED ROOM

CONSTRUCTION PROCEDURE

1. EXCAVATION
2. POUR BASE SLAB
3. COVER WITH INSULATION
4. FORM INNER SHELL USING 1/4" ⌀ RODS TIED INTO SHAPE. LINE WITH METAL LATH & PLASTER
5. COVER INNER SHELL WITH INSULATION
6. INSTALL HEAVY REINFORCING OUTSIDE FORM-SHELL
7. SHOVEL AND POUR STRUCTURAL (OUTER) SHELL INTO PLACE
8. WATERPROOF OUTER SURFACE
9. INSTALL EARTH COVER
10. PLANT TREES.
11. POUR INNER FLOOR.
12. GLAZE

MORE HOMES

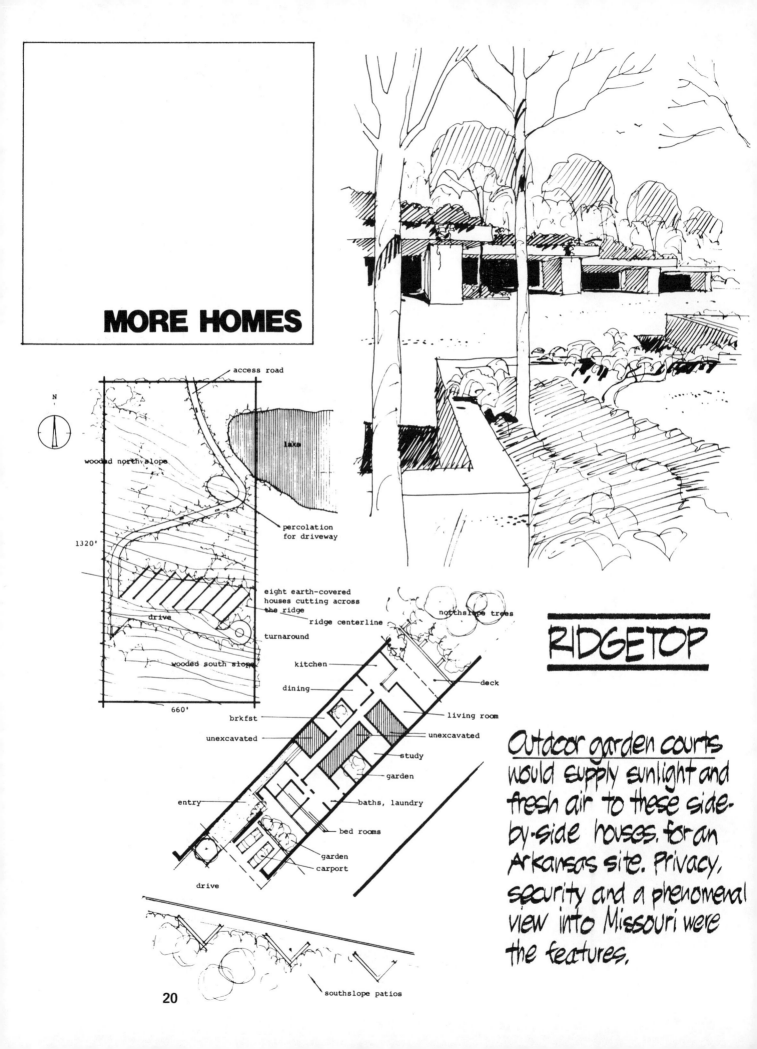

access road

N

wooded north slope

lake

percolation
for driveway

1320'

eight earth-covered
houses cutting across
the ridge

drive

ridge centerline

turnaround

wooded south slope

660'

northslope trees

kitchen

deck

dining

brkfst

living room

unexcavated

unexcavated

study

garden

entry

baths, laundry

bed rooms

garden

carport

drive

southslope patios

RIDGETOP

Outdoor garden courts
would supply sunlight and
fresh air to these side-
by-side houses. for an
Arkansas site. Privacy,
security and a phenomenal
view into Missouri were
the features.

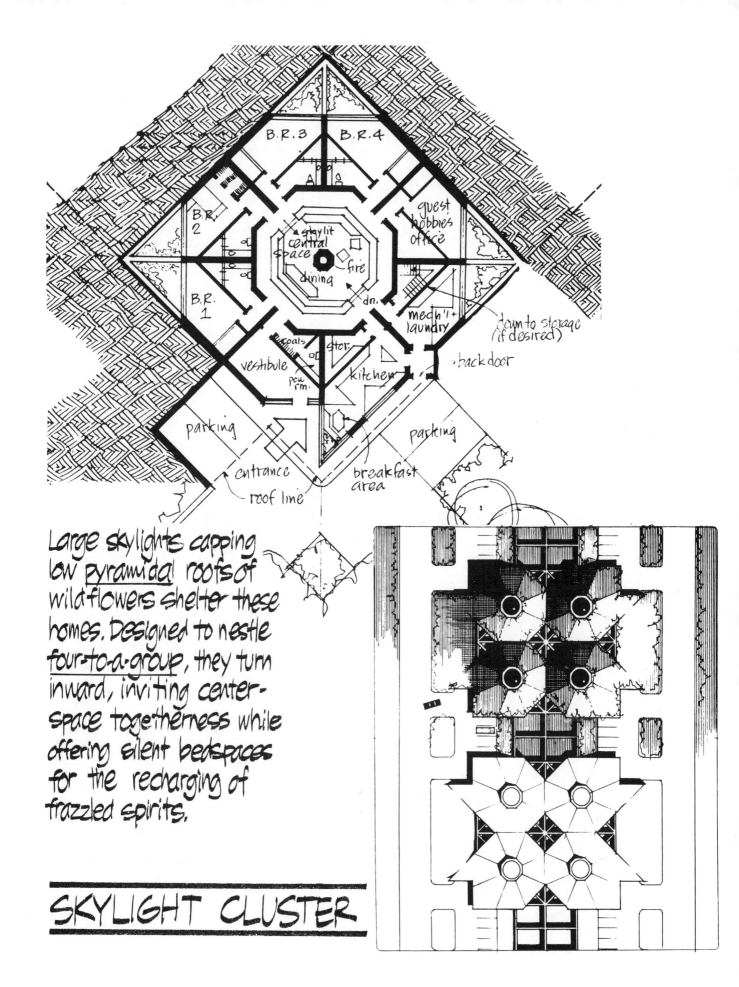

B.R.3 B.R.4

B.R. 2

B.R. 1

skylit
central
space

fire

dining

dn.

guest
hobbies
office

mech'l +
laundry

down to storage
(if desired)

back door

coats

stor.

vestibule

pow. rm.

kitchen

parking

parking

entrance
roof line

breakfast
area

Large skylights capping low <u>pyramidal</u> roofs of wildflowers shelter these homes. Designed to nestle <u>four-to-a-group</u>, they turn inward, inviting center-space togetherness while offering silent bedspaces for the recharging of frazzled spirits.

SKYLIGHT CLUSTER

NATIVE PLANTS IN SOIL ON ROOFTOP (OVER 1/16" BUTYL RUBBER SHEETING) REQUIRE NO MAINTENANCE, REDUCE RAINWATER RUNOFF, COOL AREA, PROVIDE BIRD HABITAT, BEAUTY, OXYGEN, AND NOISE ABSORBTION.

Front Elevation

PRIVACY SCREENS AT DECK AREAS ACT AS VINE TRELLISES.

sketch detail

We architects have refused to face the fact that America's lustiest housing sales are in mobile homes. This was my first attempt at removing their environmental and visual impacts: mounded privacy gardens, double decking, vine trellises and a living roof. My hope was that by moving in this direction we could in time develop permanent earth structures having plug-components: the best of both worlds.

MOBILE HOMES

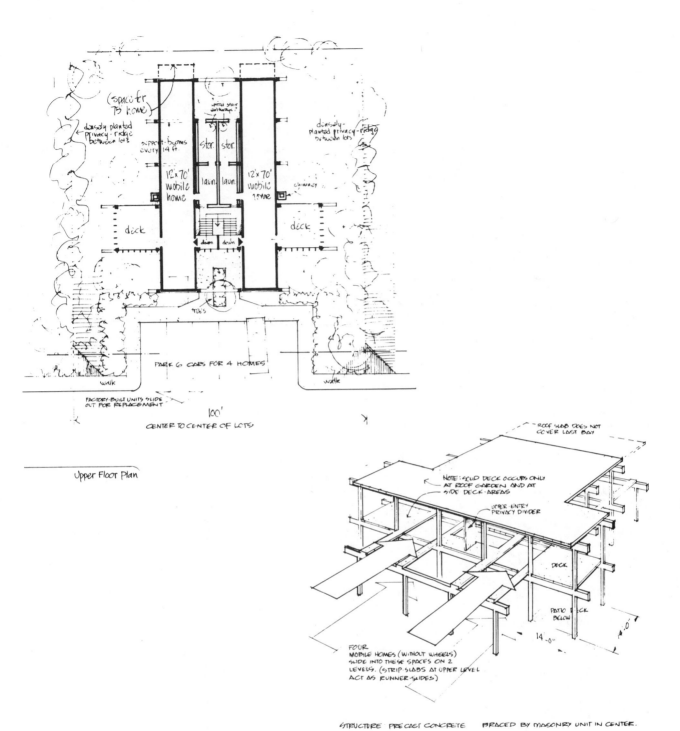

(space for 75 home)

densely planted
privacy-ridge
between lots

support-beams
every 14 ft.

12'x70'
mobile
home

stor. stor.

laun. laun.

12'x70'
mobile
home

chimney

deck

deck

down down

trees

densely-
planted privacy-ridge
between lots

PARK 6 CARS FOR 4 HOMES

walk

walk

FACTORY-BUILT UNITS SLIDE
OUT FOR REPLACEMENT

100'
CENTER TO CENTER OF LOTS

Upper Floor Plan

ROOF SLAB DOES NOT
COVER LAST BAY

NOTE: SOLID DECK OCCURS ONLY
AT ROOF GARDEN AND AT
SIDE DECK AREAS

UPPER ENTRY
PRIVACY DIVIDER

DECK

PATIO DECK
BELOW

14'-0"

FOUR
MOBILE HOMES (WITHOUT WHEELS)
SLIDE INTO THESE SPACES ON 2
LEVELS. (STRIP-SLABS AT UPPER LEVEL
ACT AS RUNNER-SLIDES)

STRUCTURE: PRECAST CONCRETE   BRACED BY MASONRY UNIT IN CENTER.

Eventually we may live in factory-built homes tucked into great earth shelters. Up-to-date precision components in a timeless landscape.

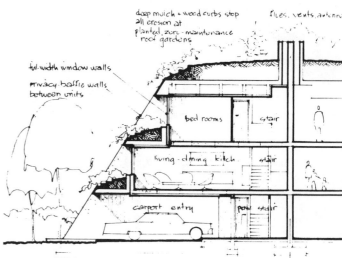

deep mulch + wood curbs stop all erosion at planted, zero-maintenance roof gardens

flues, vents, antenna

full-width window walls

privacy-baffle walls between units

bed rooms   stair

living-dining-kitch.   stair

carport entry   powd. stair

(NOTE CONTINUOUS WRAPPING OF INSULATION AROUND HEATED PARTS)

LIVING TOWNHOUSES

Urban densities, the sunny, underground way. Note that only <u>one side</u> of the second and third floor window planters has a retaining wall. The earth is free to <u>expand and contract</u> without causing structural damage.

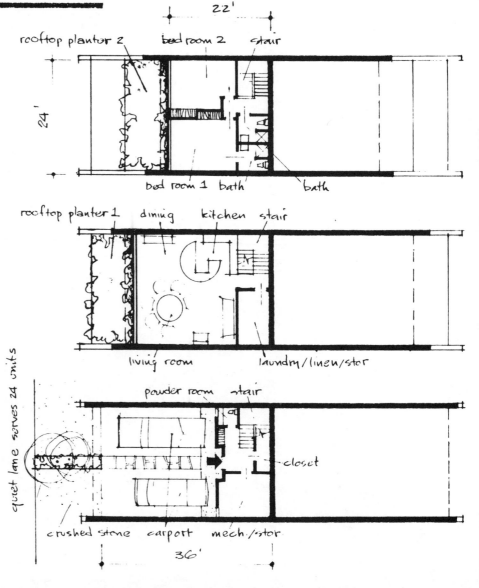

22'

24'

rooftop planter 2   bed room 2   stair

bed room 1   bath   bath

rooftop planter 1   dining   kitchen   stair

living room   laundry/linen/stor

powder room   stair

closet

quiet lane serves 24 units

crushed stone   carport   mech./stor.

36'

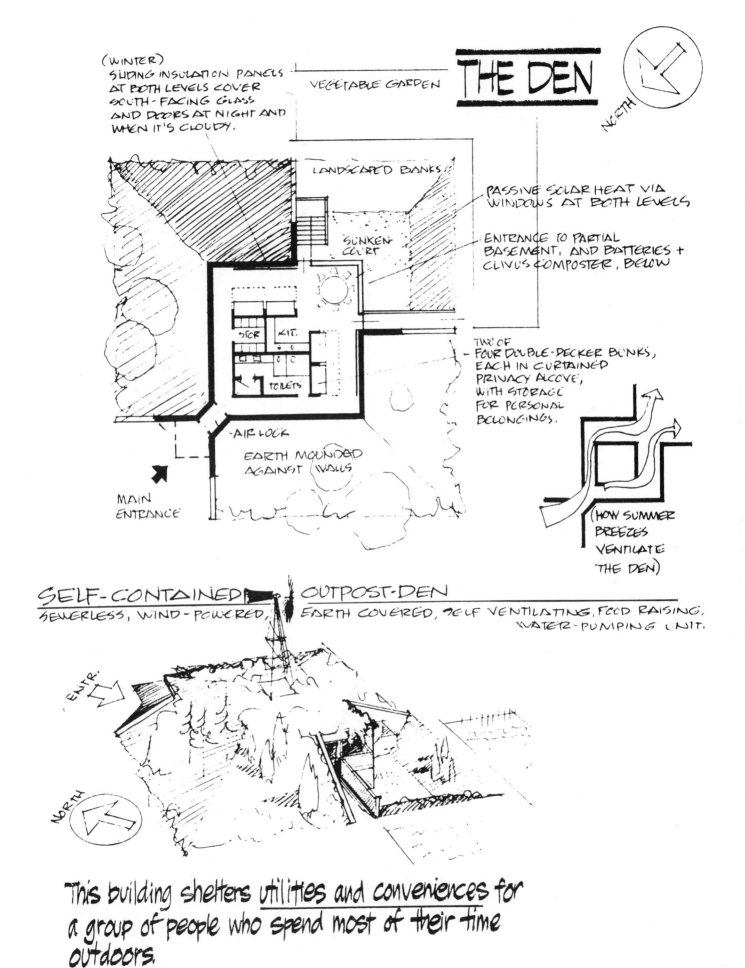

(WINTER)
SLIDING INSULATION PANELS
AT BOTH LEVELS COVER
SOUTH-FACING GLASS
AND DOORS AT NIGHT AND
WHEN IT'S CLOUDY.

VEGETABLE GARDEN

THE DEN

NORTH

LANDSCAPED BANKS

PASSIVE SOLAR HEAT VIA
WINDOWS AT BOTH LEVELS

SUNKEN
COURT

ENTRANCE TO PARTIAL
BASEMENT, AND BATTERIES +
CLIVUS COMPOSTER, BELOW

STOR   KIT.

TOILETS

TWO OF
FOUR DOUBLE-DECKER BUNKS,
EACH IN CURTAINED
PRIVACY ALCOVE,
WITH STORAGE
FOR PERSONAL
BELONGINGS.

AIR LOCK

EARTH MOUNDED
AGAINST WALLS

MAIN
ENTRANCE

(HOW SUMMER
BREEZES
VENTILATE
THE DEN)

SELF-CONTAINED   OUTPOST-DEN
SEWERLESS, WIND-POWERED,   EARTH COVERED, SELF VENTILATING, FOOD-RAISING,
                           WATER-PUMPING UNIT.

ENTR.

NORTH

This building shelters utilities and conveniences for a group of people who spend most of their time outdoors.

THE RAVEN ROCKS HOUSE NOW UNDER CONSTRUCTION

In spite of its many innovations, the best part of this house is its owners. In thirty years of architecting I've never met another client so concerned about the consequences of architecture. Now under construction at a secret location in Southeastern Ohio, this multifamily house, shown here in a slightly earlier version of its final design, will...

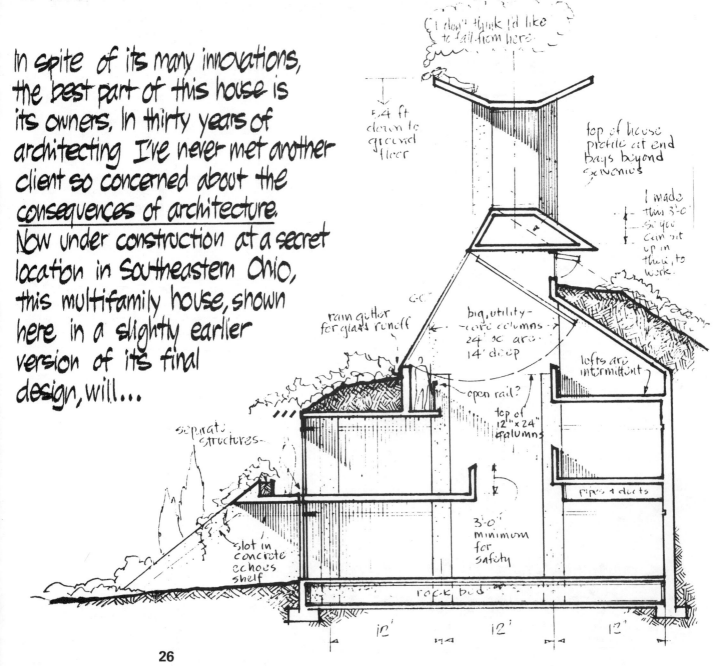

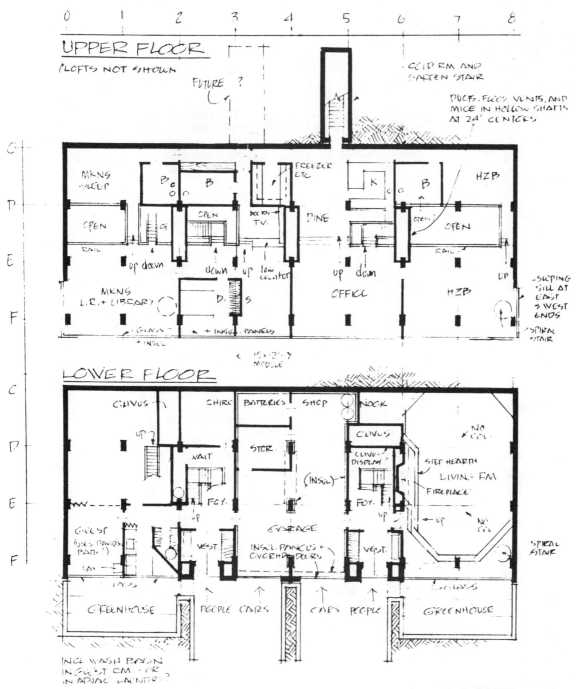

UPPER FLOOR

(LOFTS NOT SHOWN)

FUTURE ?

· COLD RM AND
· GREEN STAIR

DUCTS, FLUES, VENTS, AND
MICE IN HOLLOW SHAFTS
AT 24' CENTERS

MKNS SLEEP · B · B · FREEZER ETC · K · G · B · HZB

OPEN · OPEN · DOCTORS TV. · DINE · OPEN · OPEN

RAIL · RAIL

up down · down · up low counter · up down · UP

·SLOPING SILL AT EAST & WEST ENDS

MKNS L.R. + LIBRARY · D · S · OFFICE · HZB

·SPIRAL STAIR

·GLASS + INSUL · + INSUL. PANELS

< 16' x 12' > MODULE

LOWER FLOOR

CLIVUS · CHIRO · BATTERIES · SHOP · NOOK · CLIVUS · NO COL.

UP · WAIT · STOR · CLIVUS DISPLAY · STEP HEARTH · LIVING RM

(INSUL) · FOY · FIREPLACE

FOY. · UP · UP · NO COL.

GUEST (USES DAVIDS BATH?) · VEST · STORAGE · INSUL. PANELS + OVERHD. DOORS · VEST · SPIRAL STAIR

·GLASS

GREENHOUSE · PEOPLE CARS · CARS PEOPLE · GREENHOUSE

INCL WASH BASIN IN GUEST RM - OR IN ADJAC LAUNDRY?

RAVEN ROCKS

...demonstrate everything from wind and hydrogen power to exterior insulation, <u>passive solar heating</u>, window covers and waterless toilets.

Energy Consultants: <u>Total Enviromental Action</u>, Harrisville, NH
Structural Consultant: <u>I-tan Yü</u>, Philadelphia

JAY HOUSE

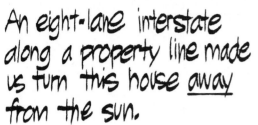

An eight-lane interstate along a property line made us turn this house _away_ from the sun.

CROSS SECTION A-A

3' OF EARTH + TREES ON CONCRETE STRUCTURE, WATERPROOFED AIR SPACE ALL AROUND INSULATED LIVING ENVELOPE

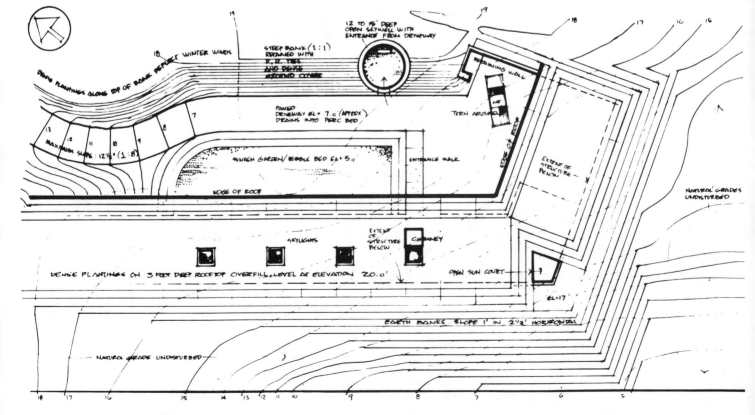

10 BAYS @ 12' = 120'

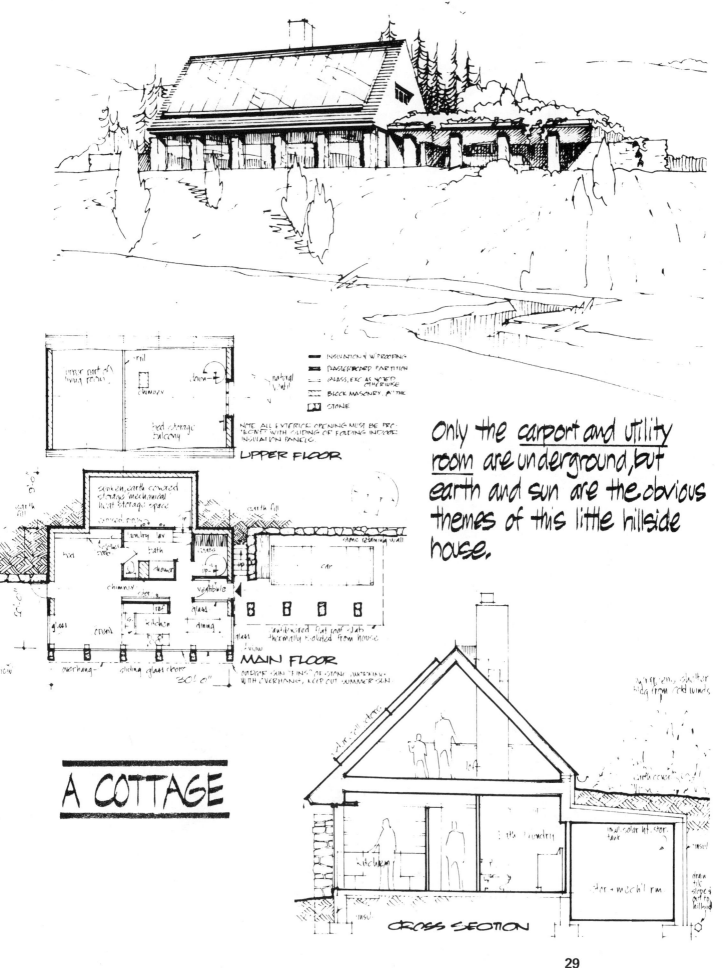

INSULATION & W'PROOFING
PLASTERBOARD PARTITION
GLASS, EXC AS NOTED OTHERWISE
BLOCK MASONRY, 8" THK
STONE

upper part of living room

rail

down

chimney

bed storage balcony

natural vent

NOTE: ALL EXTERIOR OPENING MUST BE PROTECTED WITH SLIDING OR FOLDING INDOOR INSULATION PANELS.

UPPER FLOOR

sunken, earth covered storage/mechanical heat storage space

covered patio

earth fill

stone retaining wall

laundry lav

bath

coats

up

car

up

hall

drawer

clothes closet

chimney

stor.

vestibule

glass

crawl

kitchen

dining

glass

air/solar flat roof slab thermally isolated from house

overhang

sliding glass doors

30'-0"

view

MAIN FLOOR

outdoor "sun fins" of stone, alternating with overhang, keep out summer sun

Only the <u>carport and utility room</u> are underground, but earth and sun are the obvious themes of this little hillside house.

A COTTAGE

evergreens, shelter bldg from cold winds

earth covered roof

loft

insul.

kitchen

bath laundry

insul. solar ht. stor. tank

stor + mech'l rm

drain tile slopes out to hillside

insul.

CROSS SECTION

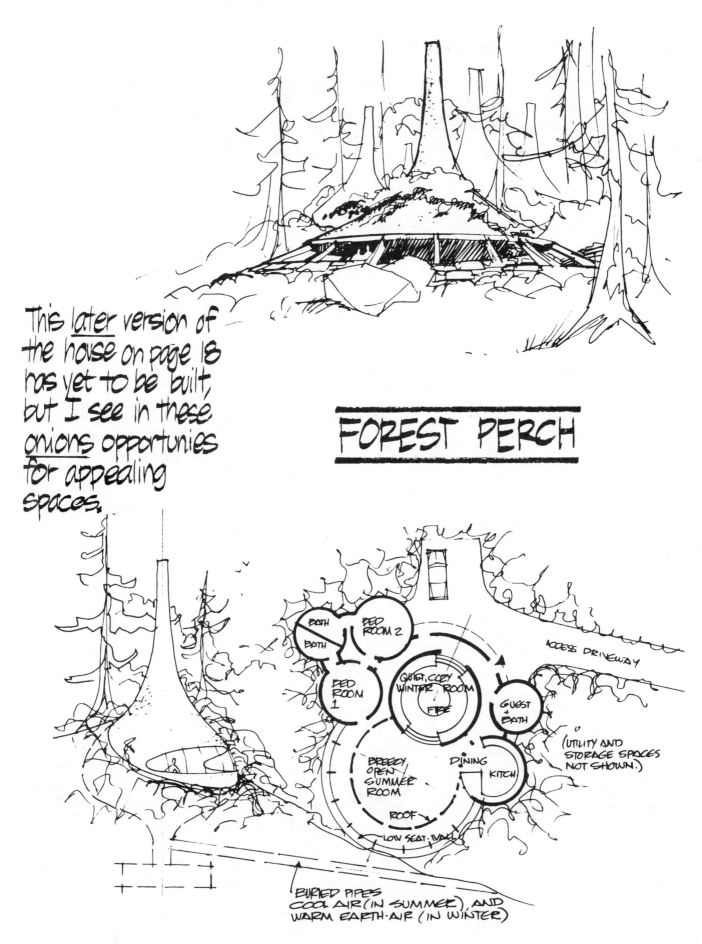

This _later_ version of the _house_ on page 18 has yet to be built, but I see in these onions opportunies for appealing spaces.

FOREST PERCH

BATH

BED ROOM 2

BATH

BED ROOM 1

QUIET, COZY WINTER ROOM

FIRE

ACCESS DRIVEWAY

GUEST + BATH

(UTILITY AND STORAGE SPACES NOT SHOWN.)

BREEZY OPEN SUMMER ROOM

DINING

KITCH

ROOF

LOW SEAT WALL

BURIED PIPES
COOL AIR (IN SUMMER), AND
WARM EARTH-AIR (IN WINTER)

the return of
the tiny house

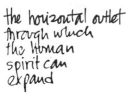
the horizontal outlet
through which
the human
spirit can
expand

Designed for <u>Japan Architecture</u>, these
houses were an early attempt to reduce
costs (and environmental impacts) simply
by reducing <u>size</u>. Hillsides covered with
these tiny homes offer an urban way
of life amongst the lushest of gardens.

TINY HOMES

the densely populated
new villages of our
cities

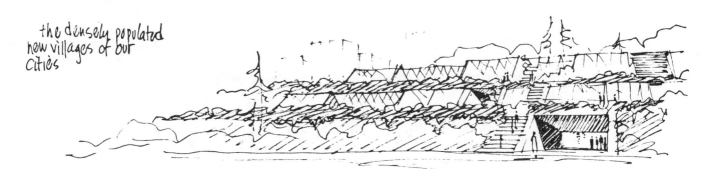

31

BUSINESSES

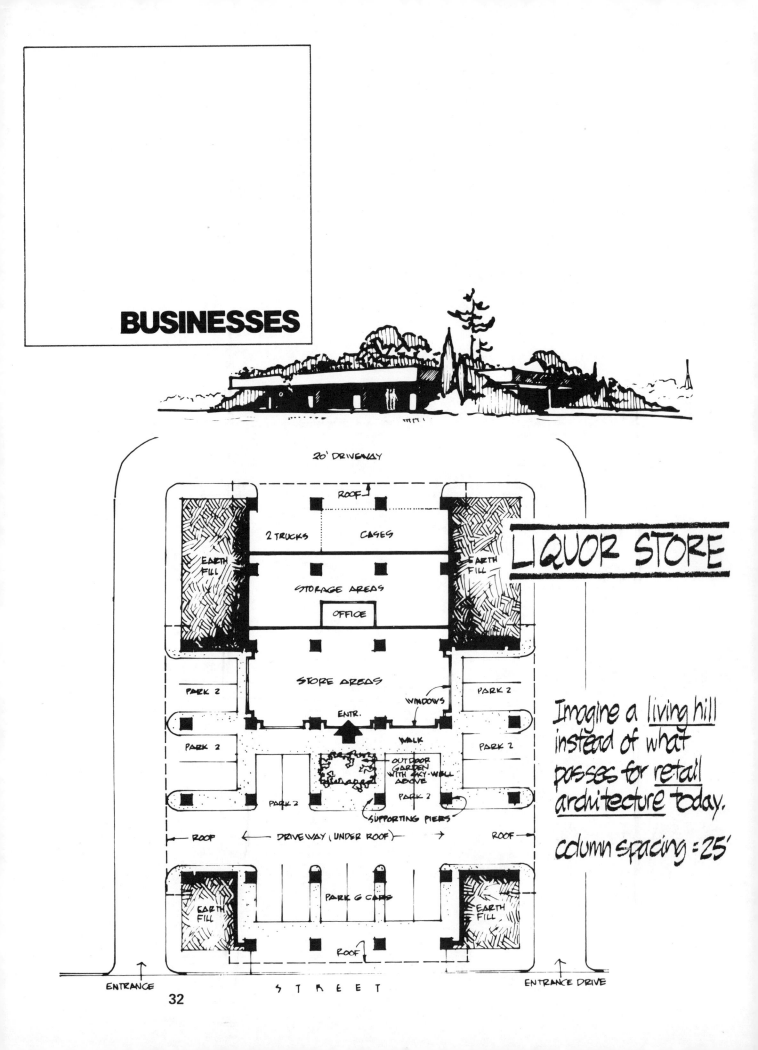

LIQUOR STORE

20' DRIVEWAY

ROOF

EARTH FILL

2 TRUCKS CASES

STORAGE AREAS

OFFICE

EARTH FILL

STORE AREAS

WINDOWS

PARK 2   PARK 2

ENTR.

PARK 2   WALK   PARK 2

OUTDOOR GARDEN WITH SKY-WELL ABOVE

PARK 2   PARK 2

SUPPORTING PIERS

ROOF   DRIVEWAY (UNDER ROOF)   ROOF

EARTH FILL

PARK 6 CARS

EARTH FILL

ROOF

ENTRANCE   S T R E E T   ENTRANCE DRIVE

Imagine a living hill instead of what passes for retail architecture today.

column spacing = 25'

CEDAR PASS LODGE

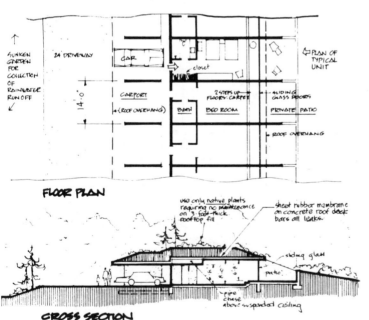

↑ SUNKEN
GARDEN
FOR
COLLECTION
OF
RAINWATER
RUN OFF

24' DRIVEWAY

CAR

closet

← PLAN OF
TYPICAL
UNIT

CARPORT

(ROOF OVERHANG)

BATH

14'-0"

2 STEPS UP
FLOORS: CARPET

BED ROOM

SLIDING
GLASS DOORS

PRIVATE PATIO

ROOF OVERHANG

FLOOR PLAN

use only native plants
requiring no maintenance
on 3 foot thick
rooftop fill

sheet rubber membrane
on concrete roof deck
bars all leaks.

sliding glass

patio

pipe
chase
above suspended ceiling

CROSS SECTION

When, in 1972, I discovered that South Dakota's Badlands were as beautiful as Frank Lloyd Wright had said they were, I rushed this alternative to the motel builders there, but the contracts had already been let. The result: an asphalt and lawn grass blot on a landscape personally designed by God.

Cedar Pass Lodge EXPRESSING THE NEW REVERENCE FOR LIFE

"spend the night underground in the new Badlands Lodge"

"See the Motel inside a hill."

"Visit Wall Drug"

"I lived with the badgers at scenic Badlands Monument"

"Vote for M°Govern"

"No vacancies at the fabulous Swanson Suite"

"For a cool night sleep at the underground lodge."

"Practice ecology while you sleep."

33

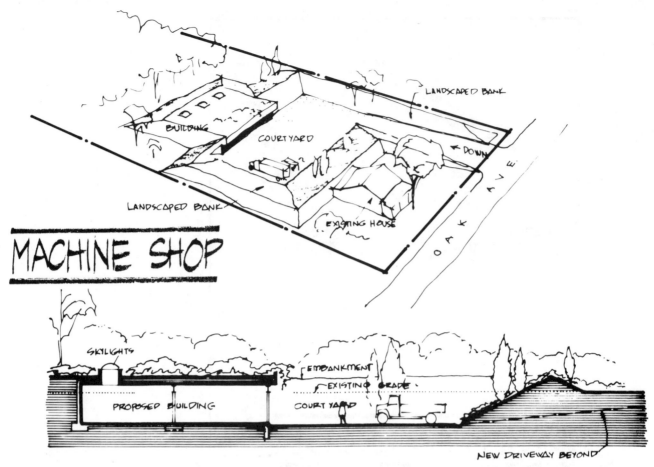

MACHINE SHOP

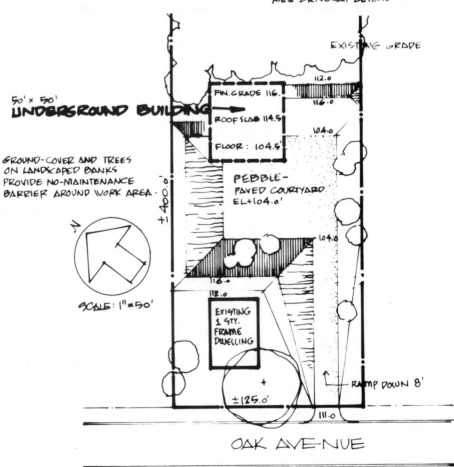

With a machine shop bursting the seams of his basement, this client asked us to design a new shop that wouldn't offend his neighbors, whose approval was needed if he was to get the necessary zoning variance. The solution: both sightproof and soundproof.

Section / elevation labels:
SKYLIGHTS
EMBANKMENT
EXISTING GRADE
PROPOSED BUILDING
COURT YARD
NEW DRIVEWAY BEYOND

Aerial view labels:
LANDSCAPED BANK
BUILDING
COURTYARD
DOWN
OAK AVE
LANDSCAPED BANK
EXISTING HOUSE

Plan labels:
EXISTING GRADE
50' x 50'
UNDERGROUND BUILDING
FIN. GRADE 116.
ROOF SLAB 114.5
FLOOR: 104.5
112.0
116.0
104.0
PEBBLE-PAVED COURTYARD EL+104.0'
104.0
GROUND-COVER AND TREES ON LANDSCAPED BANKS PROVIDE NO-MAINTENANCE BARRIER AROUND WORK AREA
+140.0'
116.0
112.0
N
SCALE: 1" = 50'
EXISTING 1 STY. FRAME DWELLING
±125.0'
+
RAMP DOWN 8'
111.0
OAK AVENUE

INDUSTRIAL PARK

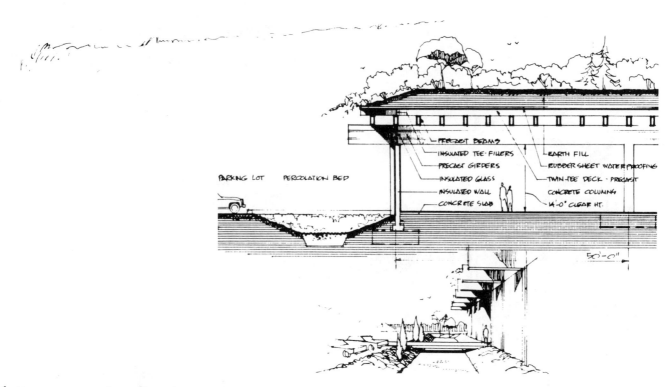

PARKING LOT   PERCOLATION BED

PRECAST BEAMS
INSULATED TEE FILLERS
PRECAST GIRDERS
INSULATED GLASS
INSULATED WALL
CONCRETE SLAB

EARTH FILL
RUBBER SHEET WATERPROOFING
TWIN-TEE DECK · PRECAST
CONCRETE COLUMNS
14'-0" CLEAR HT.

50'-0"

"Industrial Park"- the most insulting pair of words
ever to be applied to blatant environmental
failure. We tried to restore a degree of
honesty to them in this group of small
warehouses. That was several years ago –
now we go further : more insulation, more solar
heating and no heat-bleeding extensions.
The site: dead level. The water table: high,
otherwise we'd have sunk the buildings deeper
into the friendly earth.

A CAR-LESS, ORGANIC HOTEL

BY MALCOLM B WELLS CHERRY HILL, NJ DEC 72

No cars allowed. Hotel guests were to arrive by <u>foot</u>, by <u>bike</u>, by <u>bus</u> or by <u>taxi</u>. Imagine: a highrise without a parking lot. The site: a heavily wooded ravine near a central business district. The promoter tried to sell the idea to <u>Holiday Inns</u>, and they were very courteous in declining his offer. Now it's five years later. Maybe it's time to try again.

PEDALFOOT LODGE

Side Elevation

R Roof

Native shrubs planted in three feet of earth, requiring almost no maintenance.

6 52 hotel rooms on four floors. See typical floor plan.
5
4
3

2 Upper ground level

Dining room and bar; arrivals by taxi; and truck deliveries to kitchen.

1 Lower ground level. Bike storage and repair, reception, offices, hike and bike shops.

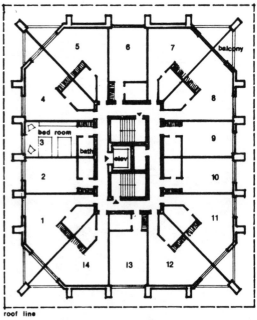

roof line
TYPICAL FLOOR PLAN

FACTORY-IN-A-HILL

FACTORY-IN-A-HILL

CROSS SECTION

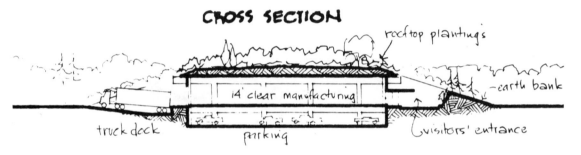

rooftop plantings

earth bank

14' clear manufacturing

truck dock   parking   visitors' entrance

It's a lot cheaper to park cars underground if they <u>share</u> their earth-cover with other spaces. Here, double-decking cut a potential 1.5 acre roof garden to just three quarters of an acre. Notice how the <u>carspaces</u> dictate the buildings column arrangement. <u>Down</u> with industrial parks.

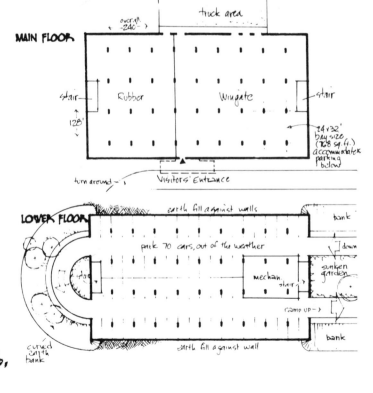

MAIN FLOOR

over all -240-

truck area

stair

Rubber   Wingate   stair

128'

24 x 32 bay size (768 sq.ft.) accommodates parking below

turn around

Visitors' Entrance

LOWER FLOOR

earth fill against walls   bank

park 70 cars, out of the weather   down

mechan stair   sunken garden

ramp up →

curved earth bank   earth fill against wall   bank

THE VINEYARD

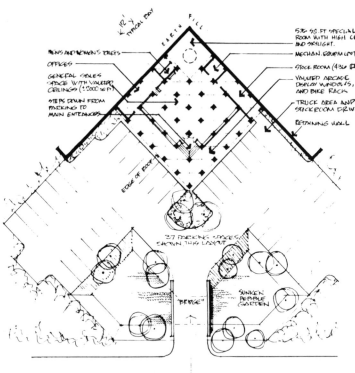

FLOOR PLAN OF 72'×72' WINE SHOP

Labels on floor plan:
- 1/2" x typical bay
- EARTH FILL
- MEN'S AND WOMEN'S TOILETS
- OFFICES
- GENERAL SALES SPACE WITH VAULTED CEILINGS (±2000 sq ft)
- STEPS DOWN FROM PARKING TO MAIN ENTRANCES
- EDGE OF ROOF
- "BRIDGE"
- SUNKEN PEBBLE GARDEN
- 37 PARKING SPACES SHOWN THIS LAYOUT
- 576 SQ. FT SPECIAL ROOM WITH HIGH CEIL. AND SKYLIGHT.
- MECHAN. EQUIPM UNIT
- STOCK ROOM (436 ft²)
- VAULTED ARCADE DISPLAY WINDOWS, AND BIKE RACK
- TRUCK AREA AND STOCKROOM DRIVE
- RETAINING WALL

Appropriateness was the key to this design: a wine shop under a vineyard, with some of the drama one experiences when touring old castles and cathedrals. For anyone who's seen the underplaces of the ancient world and been moved by the solidity of the vaulted spaces, the appeal of this low-energy building should be doubled.

In order not to waste concrete in building these massive vaults, we plan to use a very low strength mix in the center of each column once the full strength material at its four sides has been placed.

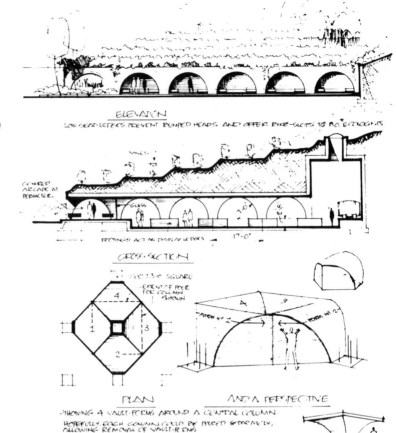

ELEVATION
LOW SEAT-LEDGES PREVENT BUMPED HEADS AND OFFER BIKE-SLOTS TO BIO-ECOLOGISTS

CROSS-SECTION

PLAN
AND A PERSPECTIVE
SHOWING 4 VAULT-FORMS AROUND A CENTRAL COLUMN.
HOPEFULLY, EACH COLUMN COULD BE POURED SEPARATELY, ALLOWING REMOVAL OF VAULT-FORMS

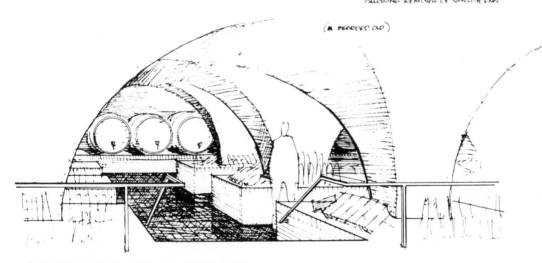

(AS PERCEIVED OLD)

FROM ENTRY LEVEL, DOWN TO SALES AREA
VAULTED ROOF SUPPORTS MASSIVE EARTH LOAD OF VINEYARD ABOVE, PROVIDES NATURAL COOLING & HUMIDITY

Vineyard

WINE SHOP WITH A VINEYARD ON TOP

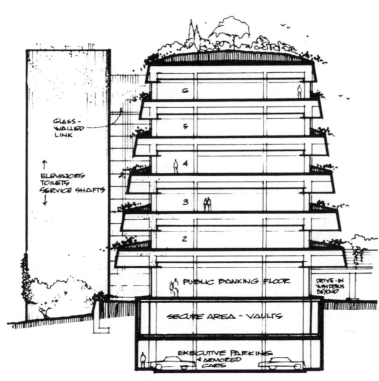

OFFICES

CROSS SECTION A·A

GLASS-WALLED LINK

ELEVATORS
TOILETS
SERVICE SHAFTS

6

5

4

3

2

PUBLIC BANKING FLOOR

DRIVE-IN WINDOWS BEYOND

SECURE AREA - VAULTS

EXECUTIVE PARKING
+ ARMORED CARS

BANK TOWER

"We've got to get this thing through zoning," they told me, "so make it look environmental."

Thus did four members of the banking profession exhibit their moral values. But many buildings stand on shakier ground, so I did this early earthie for the financiers. Underground Parking, lush native landscaping, porous paving, a sunken garden for percolation and a living landscape outside every window (we diverted part of the roof drain water to each plant ledge and selected plants to suit the various shade conditions). We gave the bankers the works and they liked it! Tested on some homeowners at the nearby....

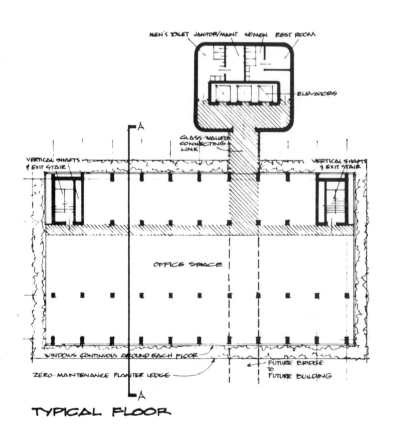

MEN'S TOILET JANITOR/MAINT. WOMEN REST ROOM

ELEVATORS

GLASS-WALLED CONNECTING LINK

VERTICAL SHAFTS & EXIT STAIR

VERTICAL SHAFTS & EXIT STAIR

OFFICE SPACE

WINDOWS CONTINUOUS AROUND EACH FLOOR

ZERO-MAINTENANCE PLANTER LEDGE

FUTURE BRIDGE TO FUTURE BUILDING

TYPICAL FLOOR

....community, it promised to win a zoning variance too. And then along came a promoter with bank space available immediately and the project folded.

True life tales from the annals of suburban architecture.

OFFICE UNDERCOURSE

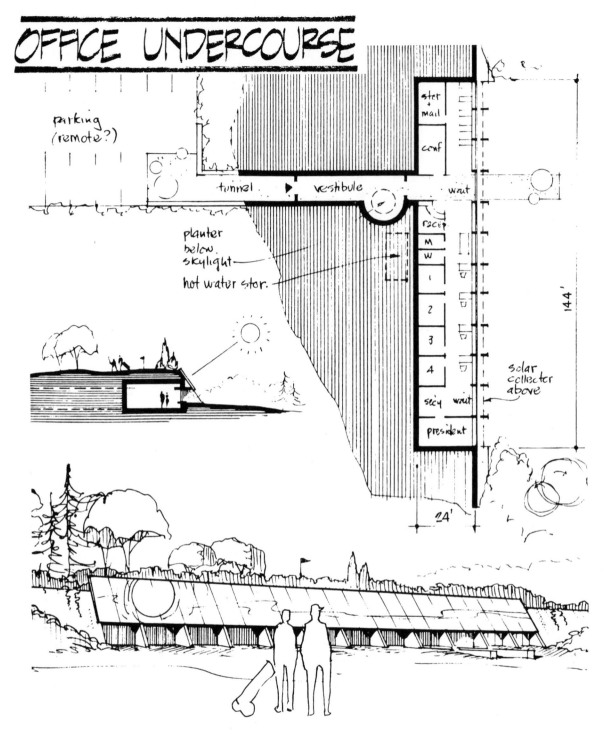

parking
(remote?)

tunnel ▶ vestibule

wait

planter
below.
skylight

hot water stor.

ster
+ mail

conf

recep

M
W
W
1
2
3
4
secy   wait
president

solar
collector
above

144'

24'

One of two designs I did for a Swedish
firm was this <u>solar lineup</u> under the sixth
tee of a golf course. The idea: to prove that
architecture and open landscapes can be
compatible. The <u>tunnel approach</u> from the
hidden parking lot was relieved by the
<u>sunwell</u> in its vestibule.

This **first** version of the Swedish office building was similar to the later one at the left, but full of my early underground mistakes: heat-bleeding design elements (fins, overhang, parapet), no solar heat, and an earthiness more cosmetic than real.

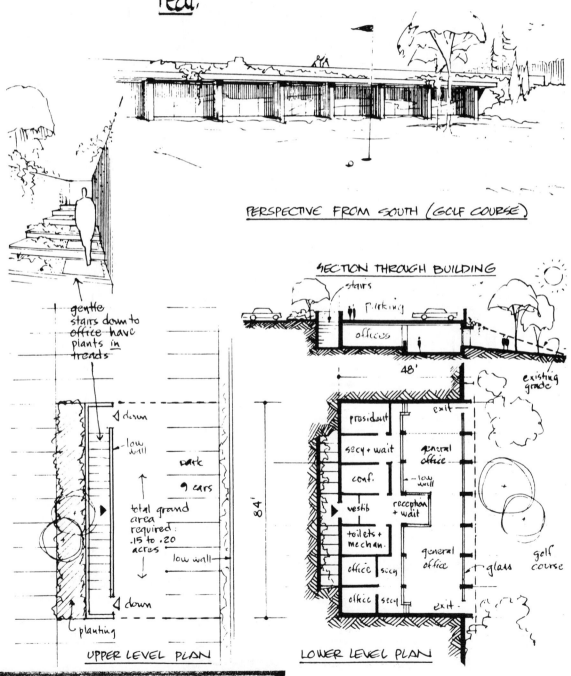

PERSPECTIVE FROM SOUTH (GOLF COURSE)

SECTION THROUGH BUILDING

stairs

parking

offices

48'

existing grade

gentle stairs down to office have plants in treads

down

low wall

park

9 cars

total ground area required: .15 to .20 acres

low wall

84'

down

planting

president

secy + wait

conf.

vestib

toilets + mechan.

office   secy

office   secy

exit

general office

low wall

reception + wait

general office

glass

exit

golf course

UPPER LEVEL PLAN

LOWER LEVEL PLAN

OFFICE UNDERCARS

43

Bosmajian

WELLS' ARCHITECTURAL OFFICE

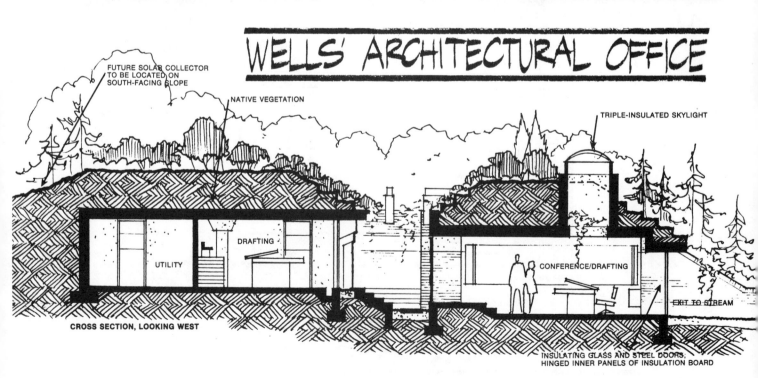

FUTURE SOLAR COLLECTOR
TO BE LOCATED ON
SOUTH-FACING SLOPE

NATIVE VEGETATION

TRIPLE-INSULATED SKYLIGHT

UTILITY

DRAFTING

CONFERENCE/DRAFTING

EXIT TO STREAM

CROSS SECTION, LOOKING WEST

**INSULATING GLASS AND STEEL DOORS;
HINGED INNER PANELS OF INSULATION BOARD**

44

I _learned_ more from this little underground office than I'd hoped. Not only did it bring back the clients who'd fled at the word "_underground_," it taught me to _insulate_ all future buildings. Still, without insulation, the lower (north) building sailed through the winter of '77 on _two small logs a day._

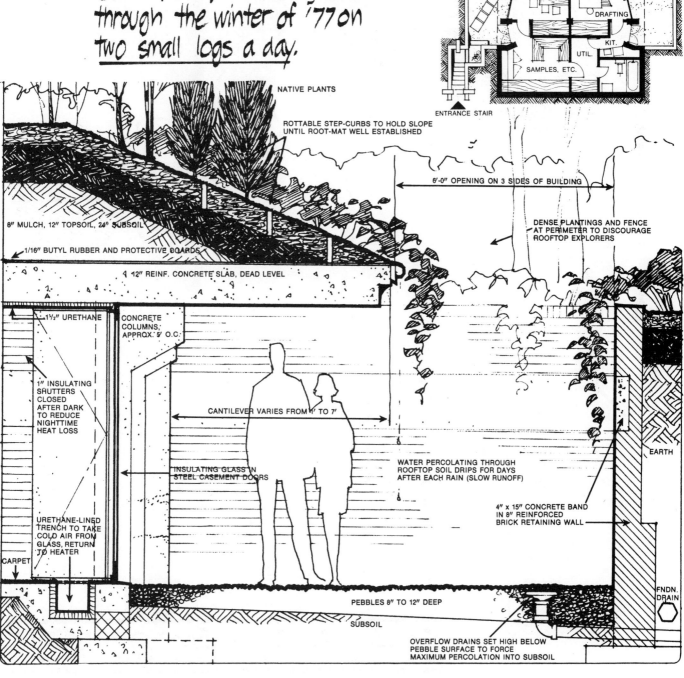

CURVED CARPETED PANEL

SKYLIGHT

CONFERENCE AND DRAFTING

STOR.

STOR.   STOR.

12" DEEP PEBBLES

RECEPTION   DRAFTING

KIT.

SAMPLES, ETC.   UTIL.

ENTRANCE STAIR

NATIVE PLANTS

ROTTABLE STEP-CURBS TO HOLD SLOPE UNTIL ROOT-MAT WELL ESTABLISHED

6'-0" OPENING ON 3 SIDES OF BUILDING

8" MULCH, 12" TOPSOIL, 24" SUBSOIL

DENSE PLANTINGS AND FENCE AT PERIMETER TO DISCOURAGE ROOFTOP EXPLORERS

1/16" BUTYL RUBBER AND PROTECTIVE BOARDS

12" REINF. CONCRETE SLAB, DEAD LEVEL

1½" URETHANE

CONCRETE COLUMNS, APPROX. 5' O.C.

1" INSULATING SHUTTERS CLOSED AFTER DARK TO REDUCE NIGHTTIME HEAT LOSS

CANTILEVER VARIES FROM 1' TO 7'

EARTH

INSULATING GLASS IN STEEL CASEMENT DOORS

WATER PERCOLATING THROUGH ROOFTOP SOIL DRIPS FOR DAYS AFTER EACH RAIN (SLOW RUNOFF)

4" x 15" CONCRETE BAND IN 8" REINFORCED BRICK RETAINING WALL

URETHANE-LINED TRENCH TO TAKE COLD AIR FROM GLASS, RETURN TO HEATER

CARPET

FNDN. DRAIN

PEBBLES 8" TO 12" DEEP

SUBSOIL

OVERFLOW DRAINS SET HIGH BELOW PEBBLE SURFACE TO FORCE MAXIMUM PERCOLATION INTO SUBSOIL

The best surprise: the silence.

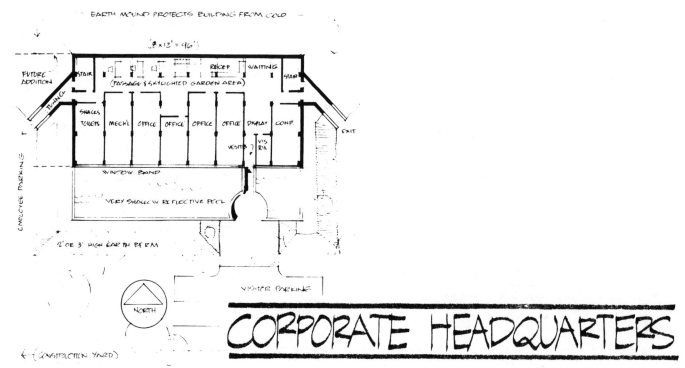

EARTH MOUND PROTECTS BUILDING FROM COLD

(8 x 12' = 96')

FUTURE ADDITION

STAIR

RECEP | WAITING

STAIR

(PASSAGE & SKYLIGHTED GARDEN AREA)

PLENUM

SNACKS TOILETS | MECH'L | OFFICE | OFFICE | OFFICE | OFFICE | DISPLAY | CONF.

VISITS | VIS RM

EXIT

WINDOW BAND

VERY SHALLOW REFLECTIVE POOL

EMPLOYEE PARKING

2' OR 3' HIGH EARTH BERM

NORTH

VISITOR PARKING

(CONSTRUCTION YARD)

CORPORATE HEADQUARTERS

▸ DUCTS EXPOSED, WIRING CONCEALED, PARTITIONS DRYWALL, FLOORS CARPET.
▸ CIRCLE IN SKYLIGHT WELL = PATH OF REVOLVING INSULATION PANEL (FOR EXTREME COLD)
▸ ALL LIGHTING: "TASK" TYPE, AS OPPOSED TO WASTEFUL GENERAL ILLUMINATION
▸ BUILT-IN FURNITURE PREVENTS HEAD BUMPS ON SLOPED MEMBERS.
▸ ENTIRE STRUCTURE INSULATED ON THE <u>OUTSIDE</u> FOR ENERGY CONSERVATION
▸ WOOD TRUSSES ON A 60° TRIANGULAR 12' GRID, SPACED 12' OC.

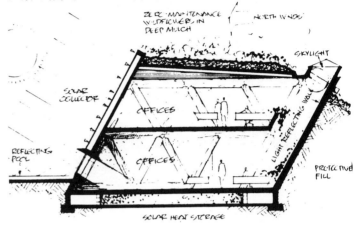

The great appropriateness of wood as a shelter material is apparent in this eastern headquarters building for a west coast timber company. <u>Ever eager</u> to express the environmental concerns of its industry, the firm asked for a timely design using wood. This was my response: solar heat, earth-cover, exterior insulation, small windows, and a geometry related to <u>sun angles</u> and <u>earth pressures</u>.

Recently, in discussing the project with solar expert William Shurcliff, I was reminded that there is <u>little</u> useful energy reflection from the pond surface. He recommended aluminum panels for lower cost and higher efficiency.

UPPER FLOOR PASSAGE, LOOKING WEST.

INSTITUTIONS

MUSEUM OF THE FUTURE

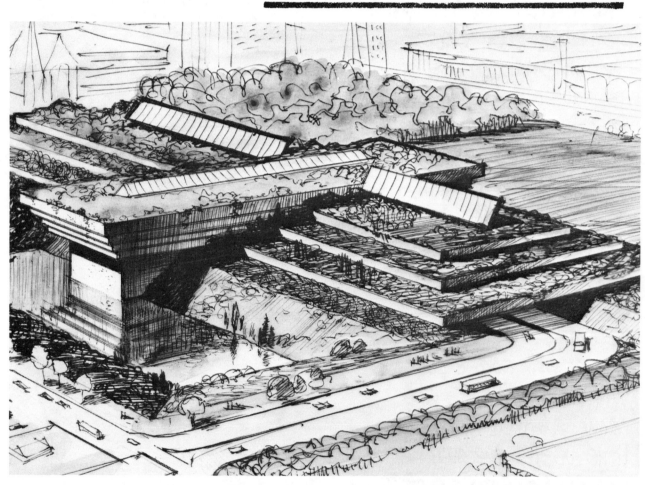

Conceived under a National Science Foundation grant to the American Association of Museums, this 1969 design illustrated the possibilities of earth cover, solar heat, underground parking and rainwater retention in urban museums.

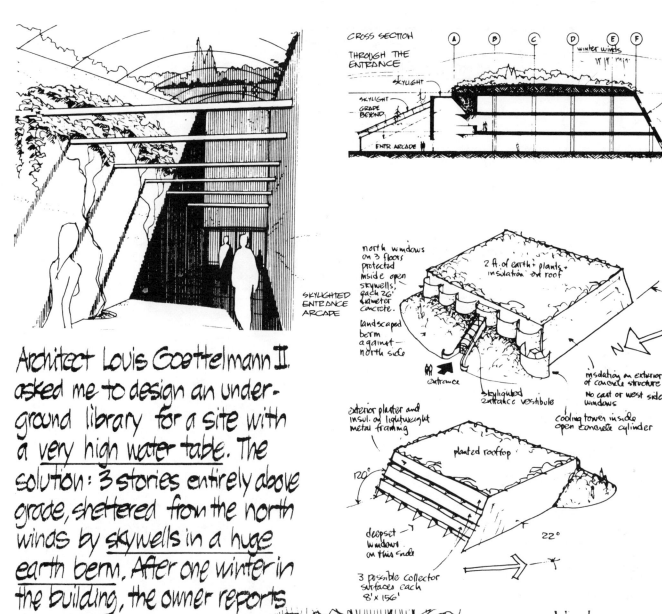

THROUGH THE ENTRANCE

Ⓐ Ⓑ Ⓒ Ⓓ Ⓔ Ⓕ

winter winds

SKYLIGHT

SKYLIGHT GRADE BEYOND

ENTR ARCADE

future solar collector

north windows on 3 floors protected inside open skywells, each 26' diameter concrete.

landscaped berm against north side

2 ft. of earth + plants insulation on roof

± 22°

N

SKYLIGHTED ENTRANCE ARCADE

entrance

skylighted entrance vestibule

insulation on exterior of concrete structure

No east or west side windows

cooling tower inside open concrete cylinder

exterior plaster and insul. on lightweight metal framing

planted rooftop

120°

deepset windows on this side

22°

3 possible collector surfaces each 8' x 156'

Architect Louis Goettelmann II asked me to design an underground library for a site with a <u>very high water table</u>. The solution: 3 stories entirely above grade, sheltered from the north winds by <u>skywells in a huge earth berm</u>. After one winter in <u>the building</u>, the owner reports dramatically <u>low</u> fuel bills.

COUNTY LIBRARY

Location: Camden County, New Jersey

NATURES CENTER

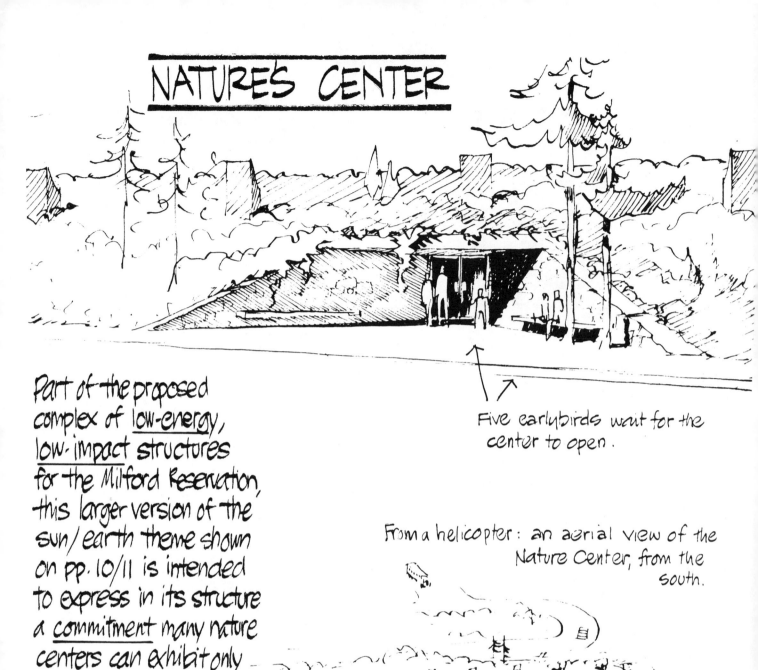

Part of the proposed complex of low-energy, low-impact structures for the Milford Reservation, this larger version of the sun/earth theme shown on pp. 10/11 is intended to express in its structure a commitment many nature centers can exhibit only in glass cases.

Five earlybirds wait for the center to open.

From a helicopter: an aerial view of the Nature Center, from the south.

When roofs reach the ground, Kids reach the roofs, making safety an ever-important consideration. Our technique: hide the required fences inside random groupings of native plants.

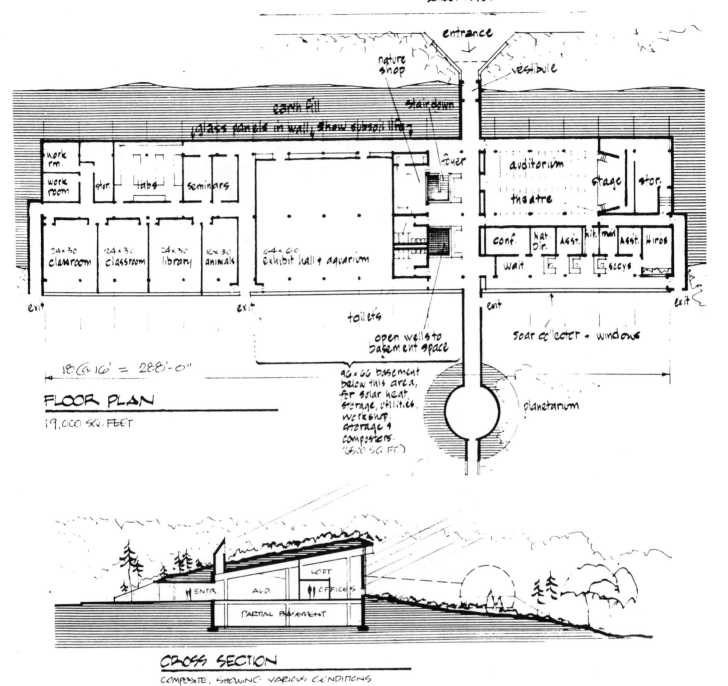

school buses

entrance

nature shop

vestibule

stair down

earth fill

glass panels in wall, show subsoil life

work rm.

work room

stor.

labs

seminars

foyer

auditorium theatre

stage

stor.

24×30 classroom

24×30 classroom

24×30 library

16×30 animals

64×60 exhibit hall & aquarium

conf.

Nat. Dir.

Asst.

kit. mail

Asst.

Hiros

wait

sccys

exit

exit

exit

exit

toilets

open wells to basement space

solar collector + windows

18 @ 16' = 288'-0"

FLOOR PLAN

19,000 SQ. FEET

96×60 basement below this area, for solar heat, storage, utilities, workshop, storage & composters. (5,500 SQ FT)

planetarium

ENTR.

AUD.

LOFT OFFICES

PARTIAL BASEMENT

CROSS SECTION

COMPOSITE, SHOWING VARIOUS CONDITIONS

Notice the passive solar heating indicated by the
lower drawing on each page. The owner insisted
that all building systems be kept simple, understandable
— and exposed, rather than buried away inside
false walls as are so many of the most important
parts of buildings.

51

SCHOOL FOR THE YOUNG

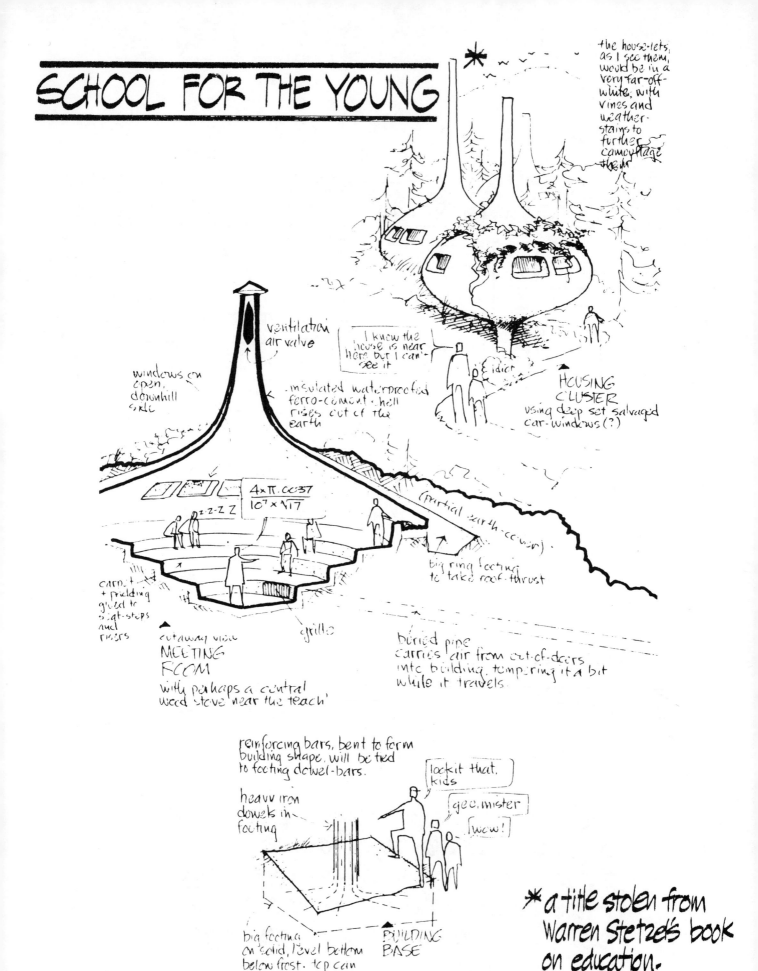

the house-lets, as I see them, would be in a very-far-off-white, with vines and weather-stains to further camouflage them.

ventilation air valve

windows can open, downhill side

insulated waterproofed ferro-cement shell rises out of the earth

I know the house is near here but I can't see it

idiot

HOUSING CLUSTER
using deep-set salvaged car-windows (?)

$$\frac{4 \times \pi \cdot 0037}{10^7 \times \sqrt{17}}$$

z-z-z-z

(partial earth-cover)

big ring footing to take roof-thrust

carpet + pladding glued to seat-steps and risers

cutaway view
MEETING ROOM

with perhaps a central wood stove 'near the teach'

grille

buried pipe carries air from out-of-doors into building, tempering it a bit while it travels.

reinforcing bars, bent to form building shape, will be tied to footing dowel-bars.

heavy iron dowels in footing

lookit that, kids

gee, mister

wow!

big footing on solid, level bottom below frost. top can follow hill slope

BUILDING BASE

*a title stolen from Warren Stetzel's book on education.

52

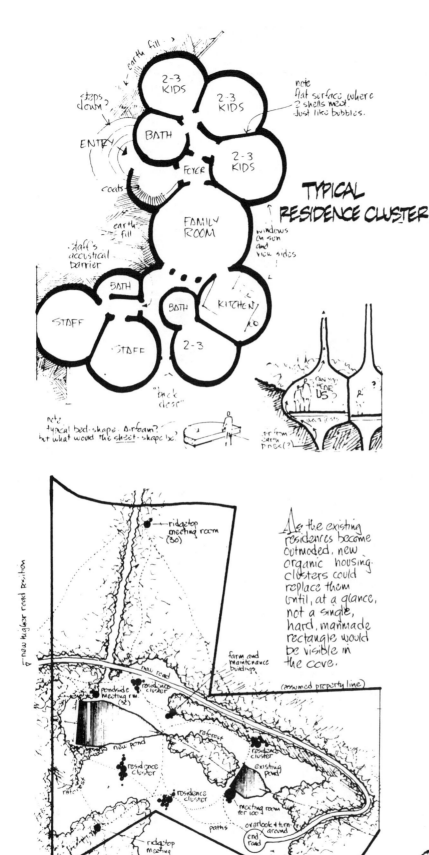

earth fill

2-3 KIDS

2-3 KIDS

BATH

note
flat surface where
2 shells meet.
-Just like bubbles.

steps down?

ENTRY

FOYER

2-3 KIDS

coats

earth fill

FAMILY ROOM

TYPICAL
RESIDENCE CLUSTER

windows
on sun
and
view sides

staff's
accustical
barrier

BATH

BATH

KITCHEN

STAFF

STAFF

2-3

"back door"

note:
typical bed-shape. Airfoam?
but what would the sheet-shape be?

CAN YOU HEAR US?

?

air form
earth
press (?)

new higher road position

ridgetop meeting room (30)

As the existing residences become outmoded, new organic housing clusters could replace them until, at a glance, not a single, hard, manmade rectangle would be visible in the cove.

new road

farm and maintenance buildings

(assumed property line)

pondside Meeting rm. (30)

residence cluster

reforest

new pond

residence cluster

existing pond

residence cluster

paths

residence cluster

meeting room for 100

overlook & turn around

end road

ridgetop meeting room (30)

occasional parking on grass.

(view)

N

The Arthur Morgan School at the Celo Community in North Carolina's Smoky Mountains bears no relation to the grim factories that pass for schools in suburbia. At AMS the kids are part of the process making decisions, helping with the work, and having some fun as they go. It was for them that these quickies were done. P.S. A cove, down there, is something like a holler.

see pages 18 and 30 for the parents of this child.

ARBORETUM OFFICES AND LABS

The Plant Science Building of the Cary Arboretum of the New York Botanical Garden was dedicated on May 7th, 1977 after more than four years of development.

Our first designs were of the earth-sun type described on pages 10 and 11, but the final plan dictated that the living collectors on the plants and the dead ones on the building would have been in conflict, so the earth cover had to go. The drawing above shows an intermediate design just before the bald roof decision was made.

As a compromise, we set the building two-thirds into the ground; so far, in fact, that after the landscaping is completed, nothing but the jagged roof planes will be visible.

Final Design aerial perspective ↑
Partial Cross Section - final design ↓

Fred Dubin's firm designed the solar system.

The location: Millbrook, NY, near Poughkeepsie.

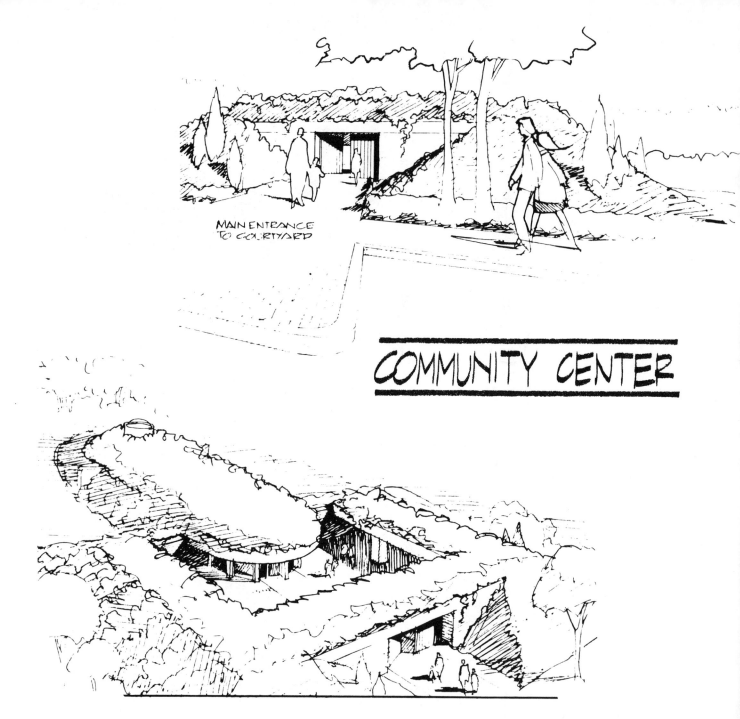

MAIN ENTRANCE
TO COURTYARD

COMMUNITY CENTER

A lovely old barn established the theme for this site where community <u>vegetable gardens</u> & <u>handcrafts</u> were among the center's functions. Vandals wrecked the barn, making the farm/crafts side of the program an orphan. This new structure on the old barn site is intended to combine <u>two worlds</u> - the farm/crafts world in the courtyard sheds and the environmental conservation world in the low earth structure.

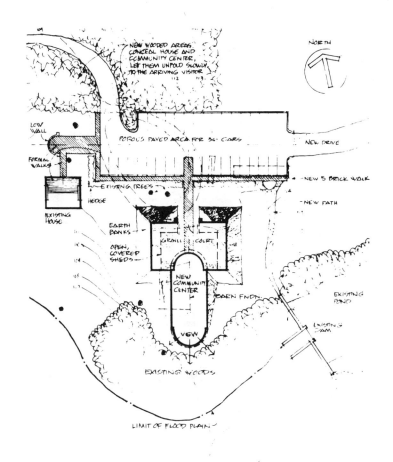

NORTH

NEW WOODED AREAS CONCEAL HOUSE AND COMMUNITY CENTER, LET THEM UNFOLD SLOWLY TO THE ARRIVING VISITOR

LOW WALL

FORMAL WALKS

EXISTING HOUSE

HEDGE

EARTH BANKS

OPEN, COVERED SHEDS

POROUS PAVED AREA FOR 36 CARS

NEW DRIVE

NEW 5 BRICK WALK

NEW PATH

EXISTING TREES

GRAVEL COURT

NEW COMMUNITY CENTER

BARN FNDN.

VIEW

EXISTING POND

EXISTING DAM

EXISTING WOODS

LIMIT OF FLOOD PLAIN

Because of the *sporadic* use planned for the structure, solar heat was judged to be inappropriate, and insulation which we *normally* apply to the outsides of walls, will be applied to the insides here, to offer the advantage of *quick heat-ups* to the space. If the use of *sewer-less toilets* is approved in *time*, the kitchen will be paired with them above the lower floor composting tanks.

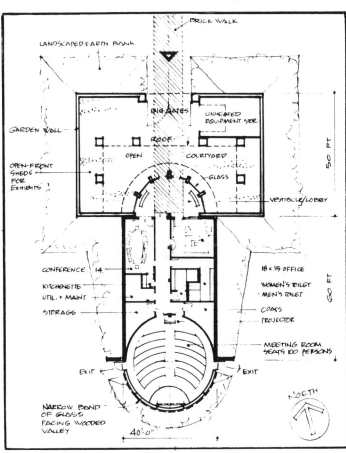

BRICK WALK

LANDSCAPED EARTH BANK

GARDEN WALL

OPEN-FRONT SHEDS FOR EXHIBITS

BIG GATES

UNHEATED EQUIPMENT STOR.

ROOF

OPEN COURTYARD

GLASS

VESTIBULE/LOBBY

50 FT

CONFERENCE 14

KITCHENETTE

UTIL. + MAINT

STORAGE

18 x 15 OFFICE

WOMEN'S TOILET

MEN'S TOILET

COATS

PROJECTOR

MEETING ROOM SEATS 100 PERSONS

EXIT

EXIT

NARROW BAND OF GLASS FACING WOODED VALLEY

40'-0"

60 FT

NORTH

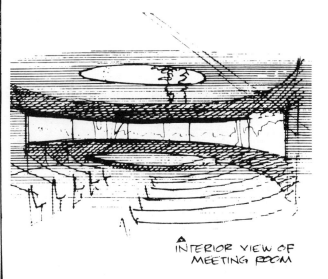

INTERIOR VIEW OF MEETING ROOM

ORGANIC MORTUARY

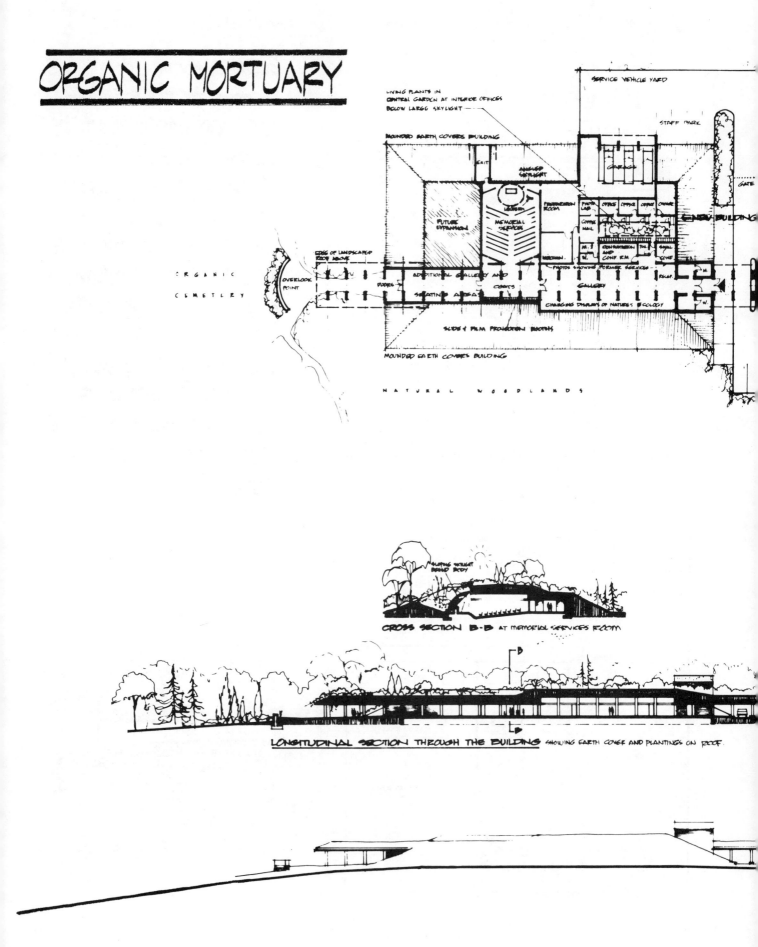

LIVING PLANTS IN CENTRAL GARDEN AT INTERIOR OFFICES BELOW LARGE SKYLIGHT

SERVICE VEHICLE YARD

STAFF PARK

GATE

MOUNDED EARTH COVERS BUILDING

ORGANIC CEMETERY

OVERLOOK POINT

EDGE OF LANDSCAPED ROOF ABOVE

FUTURE EXPANSION

MEMORIAL SERVICES

PREPARATION ROOM

PHOTO LAB

OFFICE OFFICE OFFICE OFFICE

NEW BUILDING

COFFEE HALL

CONSERVATION THE AND CONF RM

SMALL CONF

ADDITIONAL GALLERY AND

DOORS

SEATING AREA

COATS

GALLERY

PHOTOS SHOWING FORMER SERVICES

RECEP

DOORS

CHANGING DISPLAYS OF NATURES ECOLOGY

SLIDE & FILM PROJECTION BOOTHS

MOUNDED EARTH COVERS BUILDING

NATURAL WOODLANDS

CROSS SECTION B-B AT MEMORIAL SERVICES ROOM

LONGITUDINAL SECTION THROUGH THE BUILDING SHOWING EARTH COVER AND PLANTINGS ON ROOF.

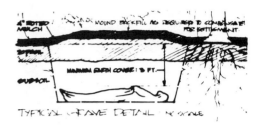

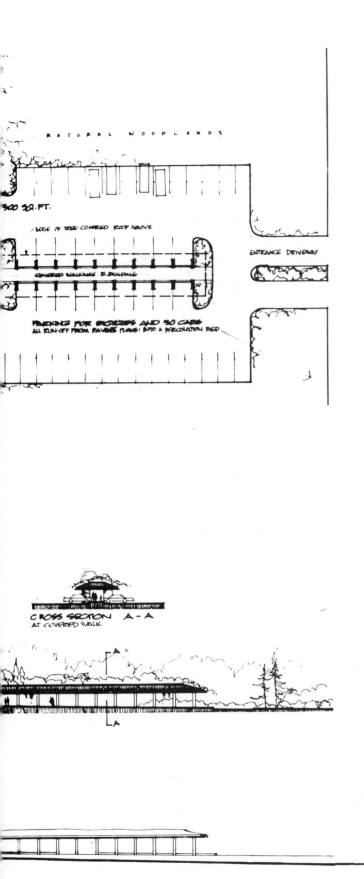

NATURAL WOODLANDS

300 SQ. FT.

EDGE OF TREE-COVERED ROOF ABOVE

ENTRANCE DRIVEWAY

COVERED WALKWAY TO BUILDING

PARKING FOR BICYCLES AND 30 CARS
ALL RUN-OFF FROM PAVERS FLOWS INTO A PERCOLATION BED

CROSS SECTION A-A
AT COVERED WALK

Down-to-earth services praising the oneness of life's circle held in a skylit chapel before a living garden.

Let it be known, however, that the architect of this design was not above advising the client to feed the site's birds and small mammals at a point directly outside the great chapel window so that their presence during services could be depended upon to help make the big point.

The project failed for lack of faith on the part of the client who felt, perhaps justifiably, that people simply weren't ready for such ideas.

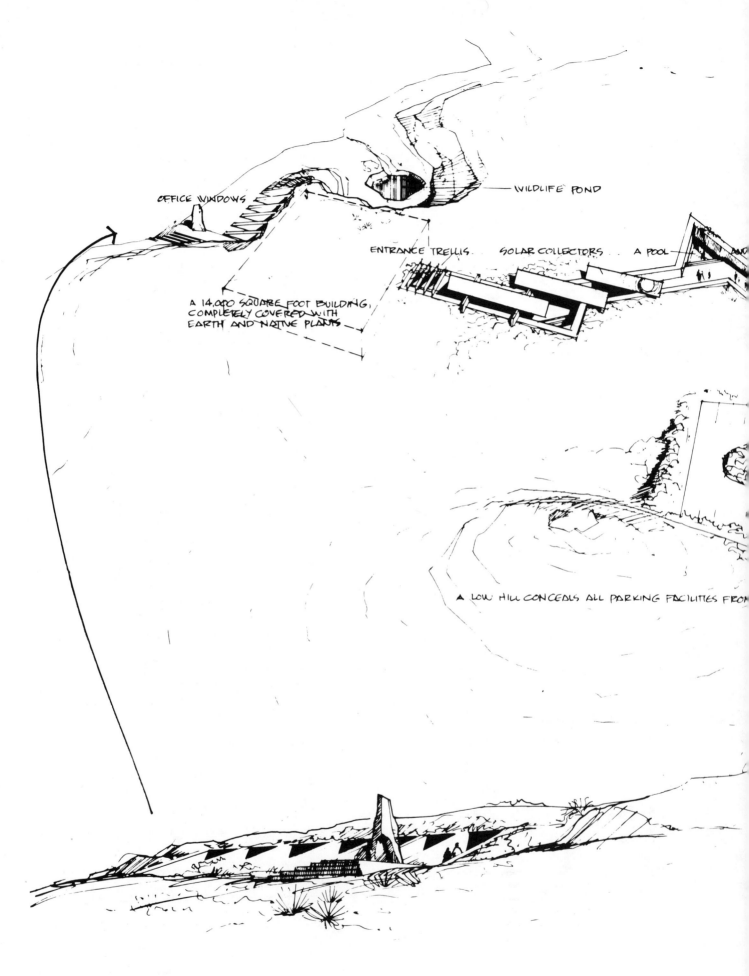

OFFICE WINDOWS

WILDLIFE POND

ENTRANCE TRELLIS   SOLAR COLLECTORS   A POOL

A 14,000 SQUARE FOOT BUILDING,
COMPLETELY COVERED WITH
EARTH AND NATIVE PLANTS

A LOW HILL CONCEALS ALL PARKING FACILITIES FROM

When I heard that the National Park Service needed a new interpretive center at Big Bend, I visited that incredible corner of Texas and designed this complex on the spot.

By burying the building I hoped not only to do all the good earth-cover things, but also to withdraw every possible distraction from the little mountain on the site. And by making the buried building absolutely square, I hoped to hold the costs as low as possible. But the wheels of government turn slowly, and the proposal inches along, not dead, not really alive.

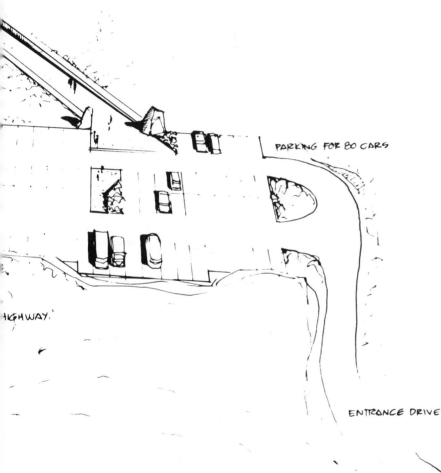

RAMPED WALK.

PARKING FOR 80 CARS

HIGHWAY.

ENTRANCE DRIVE

DESERT PARK VISITORS CENTER

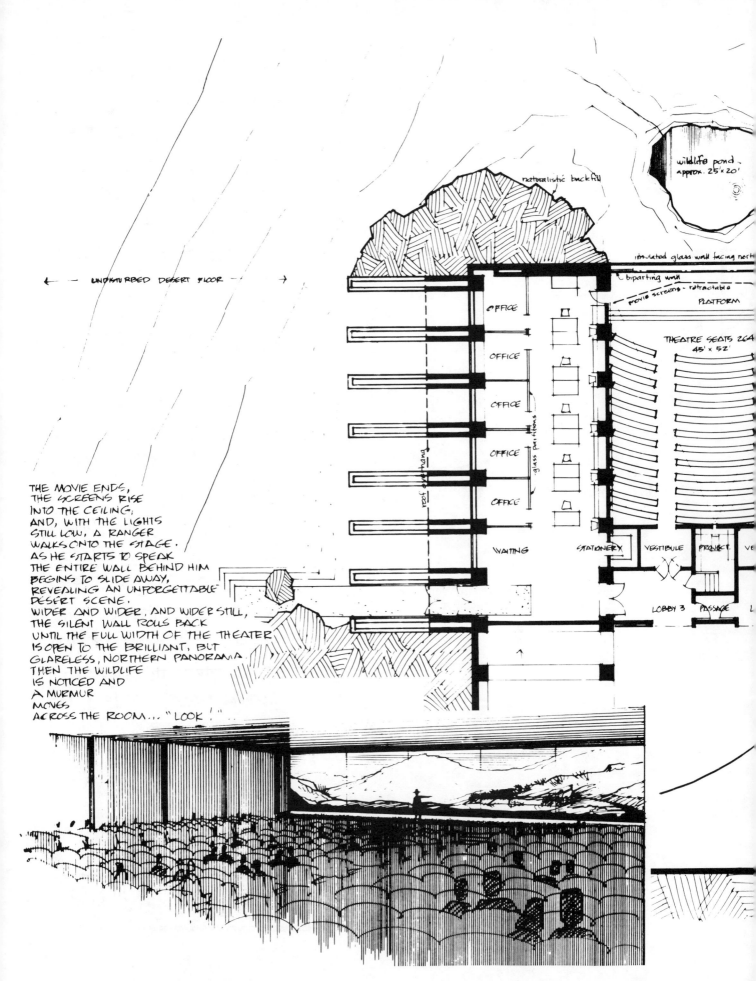

wildlife pond.
approx. 25'x 20'

naturalistic backfill

insulated glass wall facing north

biparting wall

movie screens - retractable

PLATFORM

← ─── UNDISTURBED DESERT FLOOR ─── →

OFFICE

OFFICE

OFFICE

OFFICE

OFFICE

OFFICE

THEATRE SEATS 264
45' x 52'

glass partitions

WAITING

STATIONERY

VESTIBULE

PROJECT.

VE

LOBBY 3

PASSAGE

THE MOVIE ENDS,
THE SCREENS RISE
INTO THE CEILING;
AND, WITH THE LIGHTS
STILL LOW, A RANGER
WALKS ONTO THE STAGE.
AS HE STARTS TO SPEAK
THE ENTIRE WALL BEHIND HIM
BEGINS TO SLIDE AWAY,
REVEALING AN UNFORGETTABLE
DESERT SCENE.
WIDER AND WIDER, AND WIDER STILL,
THE SILENT WALL ROLLS BACK
UNTIL THE FULL WIDTH OF THE THEATER
IS OPEN TO THE BRILLIANT, BUT
GLARELESS, NORTHERN PANORAMA.
THEN THE WILDLIFE
IS NOTICED AND
A MURMUR
MOVES
ACROSS THE ROOM... "LOOK!"

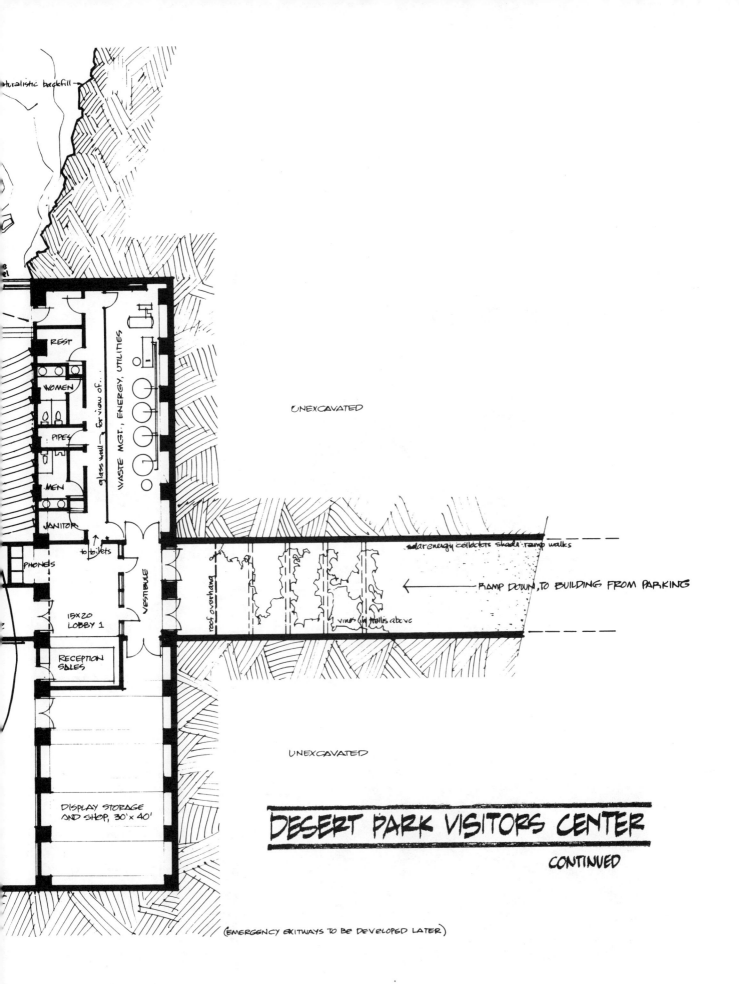

naturalistic backfill

REST

WOMEN

PIPES

MEN

JANITOR

to toilets

PHONES

15x20
LOBBY 1

RECEPTION
SALES

glass wall - for view of...

WASTE MGT., ENERGY, UTILITIES

VESTIBULE

DISPLAY STORAGE
AND SHOP, 30'x 40'

UNEXCAVATED

solar energy collectors shade ramp walks

roof overhang of

vines on trellis above

← RAMP DOWN, TO BUILDING FROM PARKING

UNEXCAVATED

DESERT PARK VISITORS CENTER
CONTINUED

(EMERGENCY EXITWAYS TO BE DEVELOPED LATER)

PUBLIC WORKS

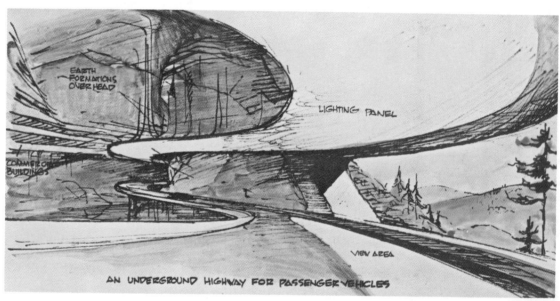

AN UNDERGROUND HIGHWAY FOR PASSENGER VEHICLES

EARTH FORMATIONS OVER HEAD

LIGHTING PANEL

COMMERCIAL BUILDINGS

VIEW AREA

AUTO TRAVEL IN A BRIGHT UNDERGROUND CORRIDOR

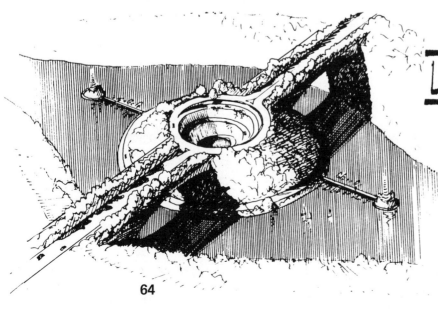

LIVING BRIDGE

the idea of land-living, flowering land-flowing continuously across a bridge is one of the finest expressions of a living architecture.

COUNTY BRIDGE

This proposal for an Upstate New York area shows the compatibility of a sweep of <u>roadway</u> and the <u>forest floor</u>.

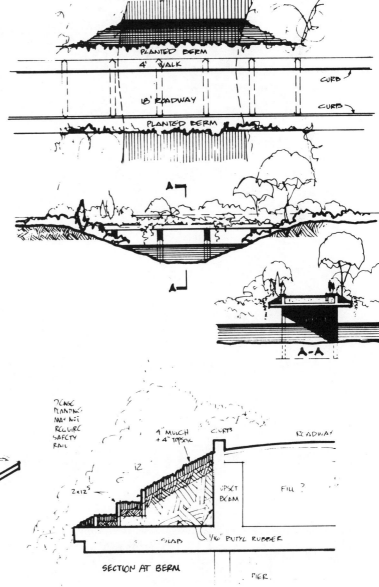

PLANTED BERM

4' WALK

CURB

18' ROADWAY

CURB

PLANTED BERM

A—A

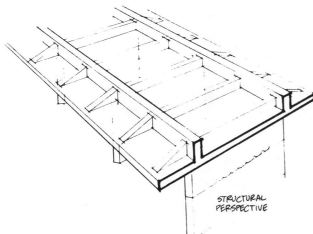

STRUCTURAL PERSPECTIVE

SECTION AT BERM

4" MULCH + 4" TOPSOIL

CURB

ROADWAY

UPSET BEAM

FILL ?

SLAB

1/16" BUTYL RUBBER

PIER

A building like this could be worth a hundred _nature lessons_. What are kids to think when their city's schools teach environmental priorities and their city's buildings are always dead boxes on asphalt lots? A change I'd make today: avoid the _heat-bleeding effect_ of the concrete beams.

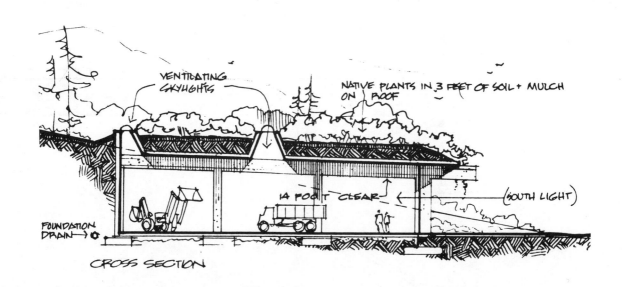

PERSPECTIVE - SOUTH FACADE

PERCOLATION BED/SUNKEN GARDEN

VENTILATING SKYLIGHTS

NATIVE PLANTS IN 3 FEET OF SOIL + MULCH ON ROOF

14 FOOT CLEAR

(SOUTH LIGHT)

FOUNDATION DRAIN

CROSS SECTION

HIGHWAY MAINTENANCE DEPOT

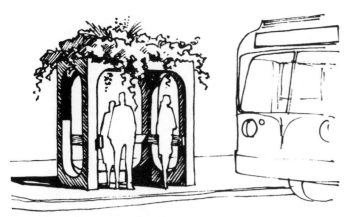

MODULAR PRECAST SHELTER, 8' HIGH,
4' DEEP, 7' LONG; GLAZED AS
DICTATED BY SITE CONDITIONS.
TREATED WOOD RAIL.

ROOF TREATED WITH ELASTOMERIC
ROOFING, THEN COVERED WITH 2 OR 3
LAYERS OF ORGANIC (WATER HOLDING)
COMPOSITION BOARD, DEEP MULCH,
AND WILDFLOWER SEEDS.

ALTERNATIVE PLANTING:
BOARDS, MULCH, AND IVY.

SHELTER AT MUNICIPAL COMPLEX, MOORESTOWN, NJ

SHELTER IN THE RAIN

A MODEST OLYMPICS

Those Lake Placid people had better call us soon again if they expect to get this by 1980. Shall we sit by the phone? Of course not. They'll never hide their greatness under a <u>forest</u>.

Well, after all, architects have to let themselves go now and then. This _Arcadian solar ziggurat_ just had to be tried. It was done for a visionary who wanted something "_everone would talk about._" The only trouble was that the people who were in charge of the funding didn't want to talk to him about it, so now no one talks about it.

150-ROOM HOTEL + PARKING

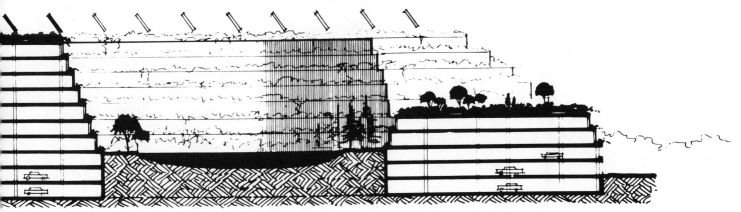

600,000 SQ. FT. OFFICE BUILDING + 1200 CARS PARKED INDOORS

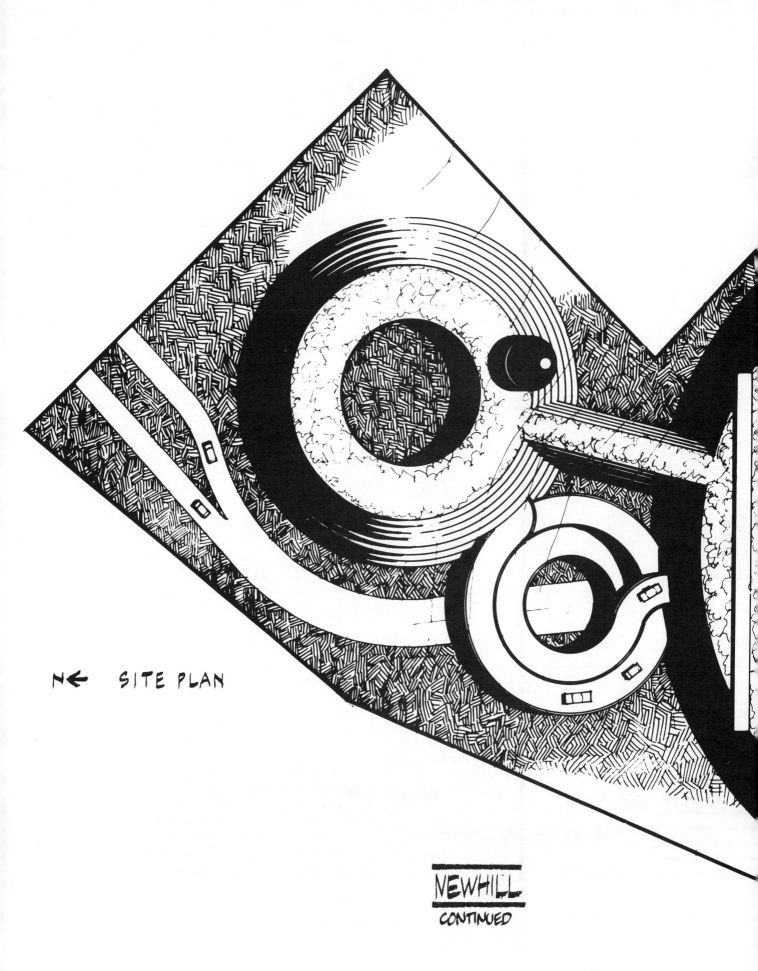

N← SITE PLAN

NEWHILL
CONTINUED

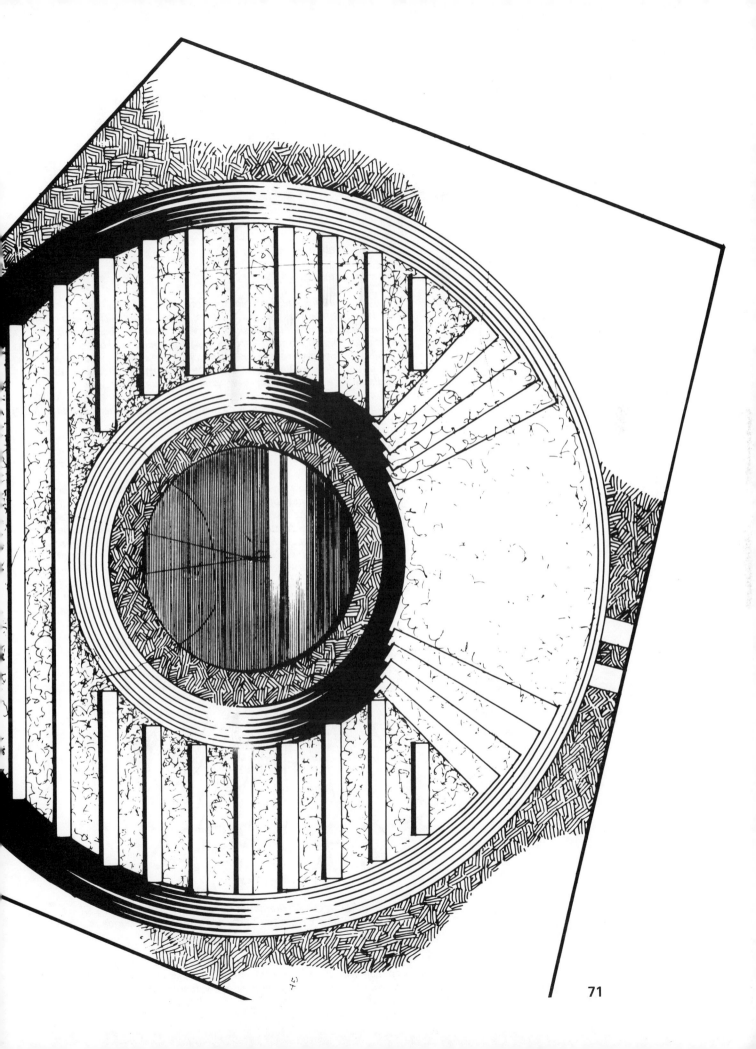

Land

Back in the old days we advised our clients to seek a site somewhat resembling Eden. "Go forth," we said, "and seek towering trees, fertile soil and tranquil views."

Now we know better.

The best building site is ruined, tortured, dying land. There's a lot of it. It sometimes goes for rock-bottom prices. And it offers us a chance to witness life-miracles as it slowly heals its wounds. The asphalt becomes chunks of riprap for erosion control, the subsoil begins once again the slow transformation to topsoil, green plants appear, sharp winds and industrial noise are moderated by vegetation, and instead of looking elsewhere for your view, your site becomes the view.

Here are some points to remember as you inspect a potential building site:

Always locate NORTH, SOUTH, EAST, WEST. Where is sunrise, sunset, high noon? Remember that the sun's path is much longer in the summer than in the winter. Working with the sun is going to be the basis of architecture's new era, and underground buildings will be no exception. Your new building will admit the low winter sun and provide shade from the high summer sun. This is important because properly designed, solar heated underground buildings may need little or no other sources of heat. Beware of shadows cast over your site. Is there a hill, a tall building or a forest nearby? They can cut off a lot of precious winter sun-warmth. And beware of compasses! They indicate magnetic North, not true North, which is the basis for charting the sun's path. The map below, called an Isogonic Chart, shows compass deviations for true North for the United States. Locate your site, then find true North as many degrees east (or west) of your compass indication as required by the isogonic lines.

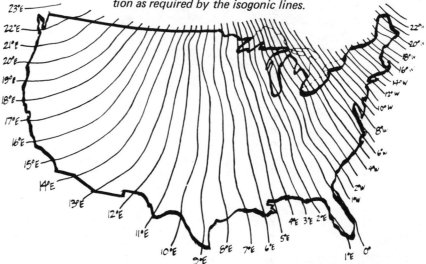

Steep hillsides can be dramatic, but a GENTLE SOUTH SLOPE is usually the best terrain to build into. You'll have abundant sunlight and positive drainage.

LOW-LYING DEPRESSIONS and pockets are to be avoided. Heavy, cold air will drain into them. Frost and dampness will be exaggerated there. And many low, wet areas are valuable parts of the natural system.

Always know who and what are UPHILL from you. Are you downhill from a flood-producing parking lot, or from a soil-fouling septic system?

Dealing with GROUND WATER LEVELS is very serious business. These levels usually change over the course of the year. Find out as much as you can about the seasonal high level, and the extreme high level. That means patient research. Although some architects do it, <u>we</u> say don't build below ground-water levels. Sooner or later the drains or the waterproofing or the sump pumps will fail and what a mess! But if the ground water level is high, do not despair! Many underground buildings are built above grade with earth piled up (bermed) along their walls and mounded on their roofs, creating, in effect, artificial hills. (Our test for acceptable artificiality in nature: do wildflowers and wild-life accept it? If so, we do too.)

If your county is lucky enough to have been mapped by the Soil Conservation Service, you are off to a good start in knowing what SOILS you will deal with and what their properties are. But that's just the beginning. It invariably pays to get expert advice from a soil specialist. For larger buildings, soil test borings are a must for foundation design in any event. If new buildings have been constructed nearby, talking with the excavators can bring some useful information. And quick clues can also come from looking at nearby road cuts or other excavations.

GOOD SOIL PERCOLATION (ability to drain) is a blessing. If the site is without positive slopes and drainage channels you'll be very much dependent on the soil's percolation ability for the natural drainage of low areas. Percolation tests should be made at all soil layers which you'll expect to self-drain. Sunken courtyards take note!

There certainly are substances known as "PROBLEM SOILS". If that's what your site is made of, you're usually at the mercy of experts. The shrink-swell properties of clays can often be reckoned with, but don't even consider the nightmares of organic fills.

In GLACIATED COUNTRY, remember that the underlying bedrock may bear no resemblance at all to surface contours.

Removing OLD FOUNDATIONS and other buried construction is costly. Check previous site-uses carefully.

How do you handle SEWAGE? The typical way is to hook into the municipal sewer or into an on-site septic tank/tile field. When you're lucky, the building's sewer line will be high enough to drain by gravity, but in most cases, a sewer ejector pump will be needed. This is no great expense, and no potential problem. The <u>best</u> way to deal with sewage and other organic wastes at a small scale is to compost them in a self-contained composting toilet, one like the Clivus Multrum, now in use throughout the United States.

More UTILITY items: Check the level of storm sewer pipes (if applicable). Where will electrical and telephone connections be made? Can the lines be installed underground?

If there are EXISTING TREES make sure excavation can be done without damaging their roots.

WILDLIFE signs may be sparse at first, but don't worry. As land-healing begins, the word spreads fast. The birds and animals will find you before you know it.

INDUSTRIAL AND HIGHWAY NOISE can usually be well muffled by underground designs. Our office is very quiet, yet only 20 feet from the thunderous interchange of a 6-lane freeway. Noise in an area is yet another reason why your site may be available at a low price.

ROAD ACCESS, PARKING AND SITE CIRCULATION will be thorns in your side if considered <u>after</u> a building location is set. The planning of all site work should be <u>done</u> in unison.

Codes, Zoning, Costs, Financing, Insurance

Every day, a few more financiers, insurers and realtors are made aware of the problems caused by land-destroying buildings. You may not find these aware people at once. In fact, you may have a lot of trouble finding them at all, but they do exist! They will say to you, "I'm willing to stand by a project that makes energy sense." Energy sense equals economic sense, today.

The lesson of the many underground buildings completed or under construction across the country today is this: legal matters and financing do not stand in the way of underground architecture — if you are willing to stick with the project and guide it past the obstacles. In many areas the building of anything is delayed by a long and tedious process dictated by innumerable (often new) restrictions and ordinances. Often these delays occur not because you're building underground, but simply because you're building.

BUILDING CODES

Building inspectors are overworked public servants charged with the reasonable enforcement of complex, constantly-changing codes. Most cities and states that have adopted building codes use one of the national "model" codes. Each inspector's job is one of exasperating detail, trying to reconcile legal requirements of the code to ever changing construction techniques and design innovations. Somehow, the vast majority of inspectors manage to remain reasonable and ready to help.

When making a first inquiry about applicable codes and regulations for an underground building, it might help to get only the information you need for a preliminary design (usually the code book and other printed supplementary material). There is no need to get the building inspector upset prematurely by saying the trigger-words, "underground construction" to him right away. All they'll do is conjure up images of darkness and dampness. Your approach shouldn't be vague and verbal but beautifully visual, and carefully planned.

When you return for a preliminary (informal) review and the inspector sees your breath-taking color renderings and charts of fuel savings, how can he help but be impressed? Well, there is a way — by having stupid code violations in your design. You won't get anywhere unless you take the code dead serious and work out design problems so the broad intents of the code are followed. Codes are, after all, tremendously helpful in averting most of the disasters which can happen in buildings. Then, if there are varying interpretations of a regulation, or possibly minor violations, you have the inspector on your side as he helps you solve them.

The big code "problem" that worries many newcomers to underground architecture is windows. Codes require windows in certain places. We find this is no problem at all because we wouldn't want to build without windows. There are many opportunities for placing windows in underground construction — out the sides of a hill, in open sky-wells, into a sunken courtyard, or in conventional building walls when only the roof is earth-covered. Of course, many codes do allow extensive use of artifical light and mechanical ventilation in other than residential construction. In houses and other low residential construction, codes almost always require openable windows in every sleeping room. Fire safety is the reason and it's a good one.

New and long-overdue requirements for the accommodation of handicapped persons should be a special consideration for all underground buildings used by the public. Elevators or ramps should be so arranged that a person confined to a wheel chair has full access to all areas.

A keen eye also should be given to requirements for "landscaped roofs", courtyards used for emergency exits, and required building-frontage on public streets or fire lanes.

A final word on building codes: they don't go far enough. Human life safety has always been the only consideration. But as our understanding of the world around us grows, we see that not just human beings and not just endangered species, but all creatures — all plants and animals — must be protected by the codes before we can say that they're both adequate and just. Underground buildings are an expression of this widening concern for life on the earth.

ZONING

While building codes are usually written by a national organization, zoning ordinances are more often local in origin. They regulate the relationship between a building and the community around it. Common zoning concerns such as setbacks from property lines, building height limits, fire lanes for emergency, parking space requirements and control of building uses involve no special problems for underground construction. In the cases with which we are familiar, underground structures have abided by the same rules as have other structures.

Since the intent of many zoning requirements is to put a lot of space between buildings for fire safety, light and landscaping purposes, underground buildings seem to have the potential for relaxation of the restrictions. However reasonable that seems, though, it is often difficult to secure variances just because a building is underground or earth-covered. A lot less time is wasted if you plan on meeting the requirements forthrightly. Here's the possible exception to that rule: on lots too small or too oddly shaped for above-ground construction within the zoning requirements, going underground is a perfect answer that's won prompt approval from zoning boards.

COSTS

Underground buildings cost more. The rule of thumb we use is 10% more than a comparable above-ground building. That premium may be paid off before too long by the fuel savings involved. Construction costs depend so much on a building's size, design complexity, region of the country and market conditions, that the only way to get really accurate cost estimates is from a detailed breakdown by a local builder or architect.

FINANCING

Most mortgage officials are not known for their enthusiasm for any kind of unusual building. You'll have to find the few who are. Impressive presentations of those beautiful drawings and energy-saving calculations help. Always emphasize the value of permanence. Your underground building — which will be of necessity built to last — will still be young when mortgage-burning time comes.

INSURANCE

Because of their massive (and often fire resistive) construction, their low profile to high winds and their self maintaining exterior, underground buildings rate very well with insurance people. Your agent can advise you on the details. Make sure you can convince him that you are well above the water table and nearby flood plains.

Structure

Cast-in-place concrete, reinforced masonry and heavy timber are the structural systems we have favored in underground structures. Our criteria have been largely ecological: concrete and masonry are very long-lived and timber is a renewable resource.

To build an earth-covered roof, any structural system will work as long as the roof has been designed to take the additional weight of the earth. What might that load be? It can range from 150 pounds per square foot for a roof with a wildflower ground cover to over 400 pounds per square foot when enough earth is used to support small trees. In addition, a building-code-prescribed snow load allowance is usually added and, if the roof is used as a yard or terrace, a code-prescribed "pedestrian live load" is involved, too. Designing for all of these conditions, which will vary according to your particular needs, is within the scope of the most basic engineering practice. In other words your architect and his engineers are perfectly capable of designing such roofs.

The exterior wall design down to one-to-two-story depths need be no more difficult or involved than the designs currently used for basements or other below-grade construction. But in all cases the design must be based on actual soil, site and occupancy conditions.

A pointer which is helpful to keep in mind in the design of the basic structure: avoid parapets or curbs which constrain any earth subject to freeze/thaw cycles. The power of expansion and contraction of wet frozen earth is enormous. Eventually that force will crack the parapets that constrain it.

Also, remember that the smoother and simpler the exterior (underground) wall surface, the more reliable and economical will be the waterproofing/vapor barrier/insulation skin later applied to it.

Dry-Loose —— 75
Dry-Packed —— 95
Moist-Loose —— 76
Moist-Packed —— 96

EARTH

Dry Loose —— 90·105
Dry Packed —— 100·120
Wet —————— 120

GRAVEL

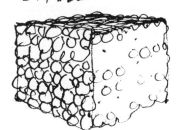

Varies — 5·50

MULCH

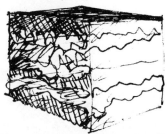

RELATIVE WEIGHTS RELATED TO EARTH COVER

IN POUNDS PER CUBIC FOOT

JILT-UP ROOFING

7 per square foot

CONCRETE

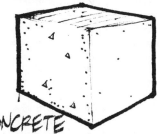

Reinforced —— 140·150
Lightweight —— 60·100

WOOD

Douglas Fir —— 34
Oak (White) —— 47

WATER

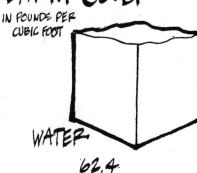

62.4

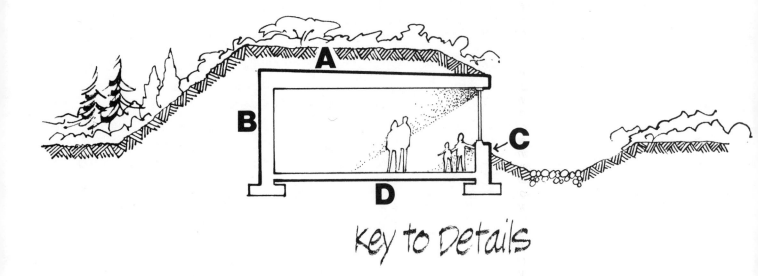

key to Details

Waterproofing & Insulating

Some people believe that the key to building an underground structure is to make it as waterproof as a submarine. That's not at all true — *if* you build above the ground-water level as you should. You do have to assure well-designed-and-constructed waterproofing in some places, but, just as important, and most often forgotten is that you need well-designed and well-constructed <u>thermal insulation</u> and <u>vaporproofing</u>.

— Thermal insulation because the earth is a massive heat sink which will tend to draw out a building's 65° heat.

— Vaporproofing because the earth around the building will usually contain more moisture than the air inside, thus creating an invisible flow of moist air (water vapor) into the structure. Remember, not all waterproofing materials are vapor-resistant!

In recent years many new materials, miracle materials in some ways, have become available to help with the special conditions of underground construction. Although they have yet to withstand the test of the ages, our experience shows that there is promise in the combinations of new and old in the following details.

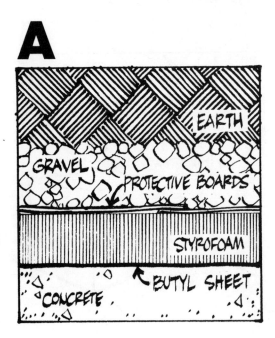

A

The protection boards are to prevent damage to the insulation and waterproofing during construction and backfilling. Plywood sheets (1/8" thick) or heavy building-felt sheets are often used. However, since protection against damage during future excavation is also desirable, non-rottable materials like cement asbestos boards or pressure-treated plywood are sometimes used.

Styrofoam is a trade name referring to one particular type of rigid insulation board. As much as we hate to single out one manufacturer, we think that for the time being those blue boards saying STYROFOAM all over them offer the best potential for insulation success underground. Styrofoam is a superb insulator. Urethane (a yellowish rigid board) is a little better, but urethane's tendancy to absorb moisture rules it out. Another popular rigid insulation, polystyrene — or beadboard — isn't as good an insulator as styrofoam, and it, too, has potential waterlogging problems. Styrofoam, with its closed cell construction ("they use it for buoys"), seems to offer the best combination of moisture resistance, insulative ability, reasonable price and wide availability.

You might have wondered why the insulation is placed on the *outside* of the structure. This is done to enable the structural mass to store some of the building's heat, thus lowering the building's peak heating (and cooling) loads.

Butyl sheeting, a synthetic rubber compound, has a good record for severe-duty waterproofing applications. It's readily available in huge sheets, like 20' x 100', which helps make up for its major disadvantage – seams. Almost divine care should go into making sure the seams are sealed correctly. Still, we prefer the seam problem to the many un-·certainties of liquid-applied waterproofings. Butyl sheet manufacturers recommend that all sheets be completely bonded to the surface underneath. That way, if there is an eventual seam break or rip, water will not move very far sideways under the sheets. Many of the sheet manufacturers supply all sorts of factory-fabricated shapes for piping and corner-pieces to help minimize on-the-job seam work.

The butyl sheeting, positioned as shown, will serve as a vapor barrier (located on the "warm" side of the insulation) preventing vapor flow in either direction (it's perm rating is .0025 for a 1/16" sheet). This will be a successful solution for many underground vapor migration conditions, but there is no substitute for the careful study of each particular case.

Remember, too, that if a building is well sealed and inadequately ventilated, its indoor humidity will rise because of the moisture given off by people and plants — and hot showers and cooking. In that case mechanical dehumidification may turn out to be less expensive than heating or cooling fresh outside air all the time.

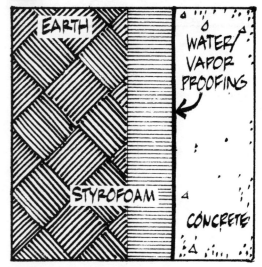

B

Conditions here are similar to those at the roof. Since — in well drained soil — water buildup at the walls will be rare, a material which functions only as a vapor barrier may sometimes replace the butyl sheeting. High-quality, trowel-grade mastics or spray-on elastomers are two possibilities.

As the depth below grade increases, insulation may decrease in thickness, but should not be eliminated completely. That vast earth mass outside will persistently bleed away heat if walls aren't insulated everywhere. This bleeding is heightened by nearby rock ledges and water in the soil.

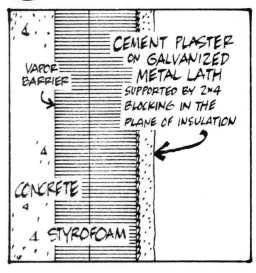

C

This is a conservative solution based on two important principles — exterior insulation and a tough skin. Many designers and manufacturers are wrestling with other ways to accomplish these goals. Insulation, traditionally on the inside where it seems to belong, at least isn't exposed to baseballs, tree limbs and ladders, not to mention rain, freezing and sunlight. And, no matter where it occurs, it must be protected by fire-resistive materials.

A reliable answer to this exterior finish problem is cement plaster on metal lath supported by treated wood blocking (2x4's usually) between the two-foot-wide insulation boards. Proper expansion joints in the plaster are essential. The blocking is attached to the structural wall either by cast-in-place bolts or by shot-in stud fasteners — all galvanized. The treated wood should be a ground-contact grade, such as the American Wood Preservers Bureau type LP-22. This wood will have a green tint from the chemical solution injected into it.

The cement plaster finish need extend only two or three feet below grade in most instances. This should discourage most roots, insects, and rodents from getting into the warm insulation layer beyond.

D

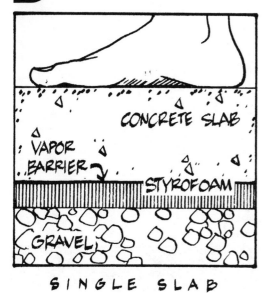

SINGLE SLAB

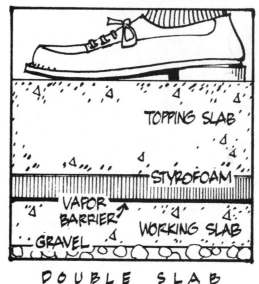

DOUBLE SLAB

D

The floor, set deep in the earth, is at the most stable earth-temperature zone. We still recommend underfloor insulation (though not a great thickness) especially if the structure is passively solar heated and there is reliance on the structural mass for heat storage.

The ideal vapor barrier here is 1/32" butyl sheeting. If the possibility of water pressure from below is ruled out and economy-measures are necessary, it's reasonable to use one of the plastic sheet vapor barriers, but be sure the thickness is at least 15 mils. If the double slab method is used, a trowel-on or spray-type vapor barrier on top of the lower slab should work well, but be careful to seal it at all slab penetrations such as conduit, pipes, and ducts.

WHAT'S THE INSULATING VALUE?

	THERMAL CONDUCTIVITY *	"R" per foot
LIGHT SOIL, DRY	.20	5.
LIGHT SOIL, DAMP HEAVY SOIL, DRY	.50	2.
HEAVY SOIL, DAMP CONCRETE, DAMP	.90	1.1
WET SOIL AVERAGE ROCK	1.40	.71
DENSE ROCK	2.00	.50

* BTU per (hr.) (sq. ft.) (F deg per foot)

SOURCE MATERIAL: EARTH-INTEGRATED ARCHITECTURE
COURTESY OF JAMES SCALISE, ARIZONA STATE UNIVERSITY

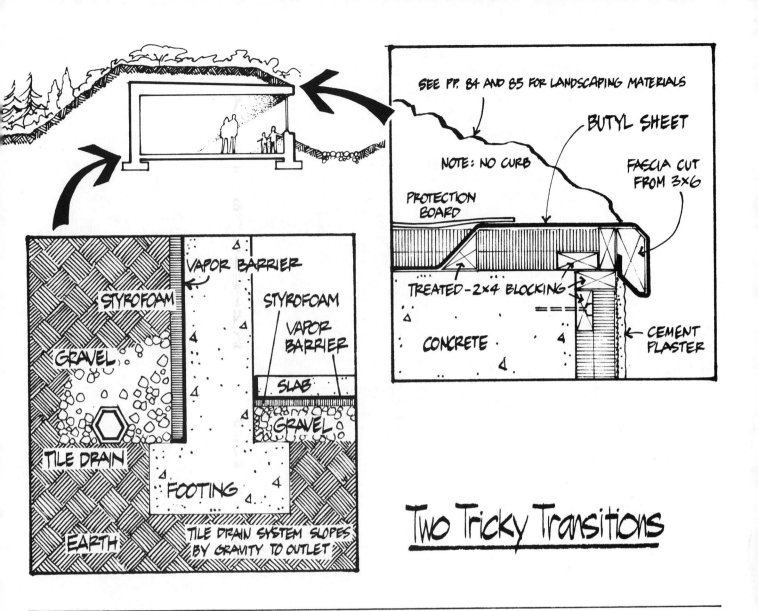

VAPOR BARRIER

STYROFOAM

GRAVEL

TILE DRAIN

EARTH

FOOTING

STYROFOAM

VAPOR BARRIER

SLAB

GRAVEL

TILE DRAIN SYSTEM SLOPES BY GRAVITY TO OUTLET

SEE PP. 84 AND 85 FOR LANDSCAPING MATERIALS

BUTYL SHEET

FASCIA CUT FROM 3×6

NOTE: NO CURB

PROTECTION BOARD

TREATED 2×4 BLOCKING

CONCRETE

CEMENT PLASTER

Two Tricky Transitions

Remember, earth is a lousy insulator. (What? Then how can the earth save ener . . .) The energy saving ability of earth-cover is based on its great capacity for moderating temperature change. The massiveness of earth acts in an indispensible way, slowing down temperature variations so that at normal building depths there are daily time lags in temperature change, and, at greater depths, seasonal lags.

The other crucial energy-saving role of earth-cover is its protection from scouring Arctic winds which rob so much of a building's heat. Taken together, these two factors account for the energy-saving superiority of earth-covered buildings.

Comfort

It surprises many people to discover that solar heating and underground architecture go so well together. But, after all, what could be simpler than this:

What could be more logical than letting the sun and the earth work together in this way? Sometimes it is simply hard to believe that so many good things could happen when we pull the great earth blanket up over our north shoulder and welcome the sun at our south side.

There is already a huge variety of solar heating equipment on the market. Every kind of company from the huge corporation to the mom-and-pop business is producing components for systems that range in scope from computer-operated, sun-tracking collectors to simple do-it-yourself panels. Equipment and parts are stocked by thousands of manufacturers, distributors, and retailers. Recent studies have shown that solar heat, even in conventional buildings, can be economically feasible in most parts of the United States right now. But most people aren't sure which way to go — high-tech sophistication or low-tech simplicity.

Our preference is for the simpler approach. We prefer to work with systems that are easy to understand, systems we can fix with a few tools and some materials from the local hardware store. If we were scientists or engineers we might feel differently about this. Notice we said might. More and more of the scientists we respect are moving toward simplicity, and, since that movement is so compatible with underground architecture, we have a double reason for endorsing the uncomplicated approach.

The simple approach — passive solar systems — uses the physical properties of basic building materials to store, and then release, usable heat. Great slabs of concrete behind glass are the commonest of passive designs today. The slabs absorb sun-heat all day, then release it to the building as it cools, and needs heat, at night. That's great oversimplification, but you get the idea.

Another passive system involves using the entire building as a heat-storage medium. Sunlight pours in through large south-facing windows all day. The walls and floors absorb much of it, then release it as it's needed. That's another oversimplification, of course, but you can confirm its basic premise by remembering how quickly a lightweight, above-ground, conventional building gets overheated on certain sunny winter days, and then how quickly it loses its heat at night if no heater comes on to help it. This is why an underground building's greater mass pays for itself. The heavy roof, walls, and floor store the heat, and the surrounding earth, with its resistance to temperature change and its lack of wind, work together to maintain steady temperatures — naturally — in spite of the day/night, storm/calm changes outside.

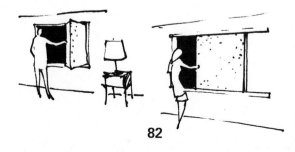

None of these designs would work very well, of course, if each day's solar heat-gain were allowed to escape back through the windows at night, or during cold, cloudy weather. That's why all our buildings are now designed with sliding or folding indoor insulating window-covers — shutters — that move into place at the touch of a finger to seal in the day's warmth. In the summertime, of course, these same panels can be used to seal-in precious coolness.

Another good practice is that of using very small windows on the sides of the building that get little sunlight. Big south windows are nice for getting direct solar heat, but south-views mean squinting; its nice to look northward into a sunlit landscape without having the sun in your eyes. If heating were no problem we'd locate most building glass on north walls. That's why tiny windows make so much sense there. Not only do little windows make the view more precious (the keyhole phenomenon), they allow relatively little building-heat to escape, and they are very easy to insulate at night. On first exposure to this idea, however, many people balk. They have to be reminded that the windows out of which most of us look for longer periods of time than from any other windows are less than eighteen inches high. I'm talking about the windows of our cars. It is from them that we see entire mountain ranges — or vast parking lots. It is from them that we see America, seldom remembering the size-difference between our windshield and our patio doors. It all depends on where you sit, so remember to provide plenty of up-close seating space at your tiny north-side openings.

Now, getting back to the subject of coolness in the summertime, remember that dampness must be controlled. Humidity and vapor pressure were mentioned in the previous chapter, but the phenomenon of condensation needs more discussion. It's the tendency of moist air to form beads of sweat on cool surfaces. That tendency is strong in underground buildings during the summer, and the sweating can be prevented in only two ways: by drying the air or by warming the surfaces. The walls of a properly-designed underground building tend to stay relatively warm in the summertime but their temperature does on occasion dip below the dew point (the condensation temperature), which varies with the humidity of the air involved.

Under such conditions, the only way to prevent condensation from occurring is to dry the air. This can sometimes be accomplished by simple ventilation, by blowing away the heavier, damp air that has collected near the floor, but if the ventilating air is just as moist as the air it replaces you must use dehumidification.

The most common dehumidifiers are air conditioners. The only trouble with them is that they can overcool an already-cool building before they get it dry enough. If you do use air conditioners to dry your underground building, be sure to undersize them in order to get as much drying as possible without too much cooling. That's efficiency, and it leads to the subject of electrical dehumidifiers. They're cheap and effective, and less expensive to operate than air conditioners. The dehumidifiers dry the air, and the cool mass of the building maintains the pleasant temperature. It's low cost air conditioning.

Be careful, though — climate has a great deal to do with all this. The American Southwest needs a far different approach to that used here in the Northeast. Consult local specialists (who, as often as not, will turn out to be old-time residents of the area).

Now just two more words on the subject of comfort: _earth pipes_.

MAZE OF PIPES

You're going to hear a lot about them in the next few years. So far, they seem to exist mainly in the imaginations of underground architects, but they have great potential. The earth pipes, that is, not the imaginations of underground architects. We hear about hotels built above caves being cooled all summer by air drawn from the caverns below. We enter an unheated subway station in January and notice the delightful warmth. And we think about earth pipes, about drawing fresh air into buildings — above-ground or below-ground buildings — through long, buried pipes that would warm the icy winds of winter and cool the hot air of summer, making air conditioning and heating far less expensive. But strangely, very little work appears to be under way in this field.

We know that a straight buried pipe, even a hundred-foot-long pipe, will not do the job very well. Its walls would very quickly reach the temperature of the incoming air. But what if a whole maze of such pipes was laid in a buried bed of stones? How about it Mr. and Ms. Inventor?

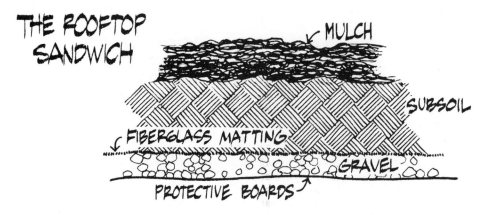

THE ROOFTOP SANDWICH

MULCH

SUBSOIL

FIBERGLASS MATTING

GRAVEL

PROTECTIVE BOARDS

Landscaping

POSITIVE SLOPES

ROTTABLE ROOF CURBS

THORNY BUSH BARRIERS

NATIVE PLANTS

MULCH

The Rooftop Landscape

How many feet of earth should you have on the roof? For energy conservation and unrestricted plant growth, the more the merrier, but very quickly the costs of supporting the heavy weights involved force a limit. We currently favor a sandwich based on a 1-foot to 3-foot soil base with gravel below and deep mulch above.

When you get to landscaping the earth-cover, it helps to look for good examples to follow. Wilderness seems to be the best landscaping job around. While our earth-covered roofs are never quite the equal of a primeval forest, they are very beautiful and successful when we keep things simple and let nature do most of the work.

Here are some essentials for berm and roof-top landscaping:

MULCH leads the list. This miracle material (wood-chips, hay, leaves, grass clippings or shredded garden wastes — the more rotted the better) is lightweight, able to hold precious water, and ideal protection for roots and soil when temperatures drop or soar. Mulch gradually turns into plants and topsoil, so until a rich garden is established and ready to produce its own mulch you must plan to replenish it.

POSITIVE SLOPES allow you to control to a large extent (especially during heavy rains) the places where runoff water is going to go. A flat earth-cover means a lot more super-heavy water will percolate toward the building roof to be handled by subsurface drainage. It's much wiser to allow gentle slopes to direct water away from the building.

NATIVE PLANTS provide not only ecological appropriateness, but also greater drought-resistance and economy. Shallow earth-covered roofs are sometimes very dry during hot, rainless weather. Hardy natives are the best candidates to pull through. In a natural wildgarden only the fittest plants will survive. They will choose from among themselves each year the species best suited for your roof. It's an everchanging, ever-better extravaganza. It's usually best to start by planting a few key shrubs and small trees (if desired), but, given the time, the remaining areas will seed themselves. What about the roots? The plant experts say that roots tend only to go where water goes. Plants have no motive to disturb structures kept dry by waterproofing.

Mulch is by far the best slope-protector, but ROTTABLE ROOF CURBS provide additional temporary protection at roof edges, allowing time for root networks to become established and help stabilize slopes. Curb materials cost nothing since you can use waste boards left over from construction. The wood will quickly blend in with the plantings.

THORNY BUSH BARRIERS take on a double role as safety fences, protecting high roof edges from falling children, and, as natural green cover, adding wildlife cover. A sturdy artificial protective fence must usually be used to protect unsuspecting persons from stepping off the edge of the roof, but it can be made almost invisible if it's painted (mix green, black and brown to obtain the average local winter landscape color), and by locating it inconspicuously, away from the roof edge, also by zig-zagging it among random shrubs (rather than straight-lining it to form a repulsive outdoor box-space).

As landscape decisions are made affecting not only the roof but the entire site, more and more people are opting for these ecological guidelines:

When choosing new plants — shrubs and trees — stay away from the strictly ornamental varieties. Select FOOD-BEARING PLANTS — fruit trees, raspberry bushes, blueberries.

Always provide some WILDLIFE COVER, even if it's no more than a brushpile. Open basins can provide much-needed drinking water for birds and small animals. Now that you've gone this far, it takes only a little research to find out what particular planting will provide a wildlife food source more popular than your vegetable garden.

A PERCOLATION BED is a fancy way of saying a big shallow pit with a gravel floor for soaking up excess raindrops. But what a difference it makes in retaining and controlling runoff! Instead of causing erosion and flash flooding, rain water drained into a percolation bed does the job it was meant to do. If it's possible on your site, see that all construction-area runoff is directed into one (or more) of these beds.

COMPOSTING involves the natural decomposition of organic matter (anything from leaves to kitchen scraps — leave out the meat, please) into life-giving humus, one of the soil's vital parts. After being exposed to all the years of examples in magazines like Organic Gardening and Farming there's just not any excuse now for not putting your garbage to work. The choice of techniques ranges from no-cost piling methods to convenient prefab bins.

YOUR VEGETABLE GARDEN is where all that compost will be put to work. Carefully locate the garden — not in some left-over spot — but where the soil's best, where there's full sunlight and good drainage, and where you can reach it from the kitchen as easily as possible. A prediction: vegetable gardens will begin to spring up at work places like small businesses and offices. It's a good way to get lunch-hour sun and exercise and put those monotonous lawns to work.

POROUS PAVING is the ecologically-sensible way to surface long-lasting parking and driveway areas. It consists, simply, of special perforated precast blocks hand-laid on a gravel bed. Usually, the holes in the blocks are filled with soil which will soon support a luxuriant plant cover. The result: a handsome hard surface capable of handling the loads of heavy trucks, but with grass and plants popping up all over. And rain will gently drain through it.

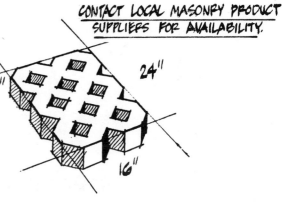

CONTACT LOCAL MASONRY PRODUCT SUPPLIERS FOR AVAILABILITY.

24"

5"

16"

Commercially-done porous paving installations are expensive, but they can often go a long way toward paying for themselves through special consideration from planning commissions (fewer drain pipes required) and upgrading a project's looks (imagine a grassy truck depot). They are ideal as a do-it-yourself production since most of the costs are in the labor.

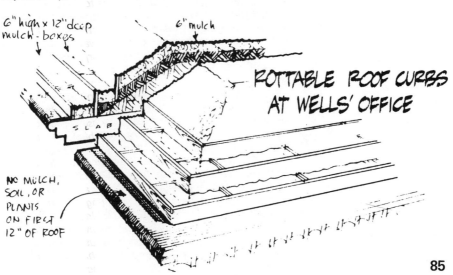

6" high x 12" deep mulch-boxes

6" mulch

SLAB

ROTTABLE ROOF CURBS AT WELLS' OFFICE

NO MULCH, SOIL, OR PLANTS ON FIRST 12" OF ROOF

Secrets

Part of the reason underground architecture is so fascinating today is that once you get involved in it, it's like being in a secret society. Besides exciting the curiosity of your neighbors, and building new bonds of friendship with fellow energy-saving underground dwellers, you also begin to hear about the ancient lost scrolls of underground building wisdom.

Well, just about. It is amazing how inaccessible and unpublicized a lot of information in the field really is. Frequently we hear people say, in desperation, "I've looked everywhere and can't find information on underground architecture." Others will say in an almost mysterious tone: "The literature in this field is obscurely scattered." When news of underground architecture bibliographies first appeared, those lists were sought out as rare treasure.

Now, things are improving — thanks in part to this book (Right? Right!) and thanks in part to all the articles now appearing in national magazines. Still the question arises: Where should you go from here for the next step toward realizing your building?

In response to all the requests I've had for house plans and details my architect son and I have produced an oversized (22'' x 11'') 44 - page paperback showing 8 different underground house plans at large scale along with many pages of information and details.

Underground Plans Book 1
By Malcolm Wells and Sam Glenn-Wells

from: Malcolm Wells P.O. Box 1149
      Brewster, MA 02631

$13.00 postpaid

Our favorite general article on why to build with earth-cover (in case you're looking for the final touch to convince your Aunt Harriet) is this ten page one, profusely illustrated:

    "Underground Architecture"
    by Malcolm Wells
    in CoEvolution Quarterly, Fall 1976

    from:

    Malcolm Wells
    P.O. Box 1149
    Brewster, MA 02631

    $2.50

An excellent source of general and specific information is a big, 8½'' x 11'', 310-page paperback, crammed with design and energy topics, structural and waterproofing facts; code, zoning, and financial sections, illustrative designs with photos of many houses, and appendices packed with tables, graphs, and sources of further information. Written by the people at The Underground Space Center of the University of Minnesota, it contains only five (out of hundreds of) subjects with which I disagree, and, with the USC's kind permission, I offer the book for sale along with my 4-page, illustrated critique covering those five disputed subjects.

    Earth Sheltered Housing Design

    from:
    Malcolm Wells
    P.O. Box 1149
    Brewster, MA 02631

    $14.00 postpaid

Postscript

ARCHITECTURAL SERVICES. I can provide them for only a few selected projects each year. My advice is to find a local architect whose work pleases you, interview him or her, and, if you think a harmonious relationship is likely, engage him or her to do the job. If the underground rules are followed, everything should go pretty well, although all building projects have their share of unpleasant surprises. The key to success is extreme care in the structural, waterproofing, insulating, and backfilling work.

If you don't know of any local architects, get in touch with the American Institute of Architects, 1735 New York Avenue NW, Washington, DC 20006, for a listing of those in your area.

Good luck!

MALCOLM WELLS